D0977162

CLIMB
A
FALLEN
LADDER

CLIMB A FALLEN LADDER

How to Survive (and Thrive!)
in a Downsized America

Rochelle H. Gordon, M.D.
and
Catherine E. Harold

Hatherleigh Press

New York

Hatherleigh Press
1114 First Avenue
New York, NY 10021

The patients represented in this book are composites of many people and ideas. They do not represent specific individuals, either living or dead.

The ideas and suggestions contained in this book are not intended as a substitute for consulting with a physician. All matters regarding your health require medical supervision.

Library of Congress Cataloging-in-Publication Data
Gordon, Rochelle H., 1945–
    Climb a fallen ladder: how to survive (and thrive) in a
downsized America/Rochelle H. Gordon and Catherine E.
Harold.
        p.   cm.
Includes bibliographical references and index.
        ISBN 1-886330-96-4 (hardcover: alk. paper)
        1. Unemployed—Life skills guides. 2. Displaced workers—
Life skills guides. 3. Unemployed—Psychology. 4. Displaced
workers—Psychology. 5. Unemployment—Psychological aspects.
6. Downsizing of organizations—Psychological aspects.
I. Harold, Catherine E., 1957–   . II. Title.
HD5708.G67   1997
158.1—dc21   96-47829
CIP

Designed by Dede Cummings

Printed in the United States of America on acid-free paper ♾

10 9 8 7 6 5 4 3 2 1

*This book is dedicated to the patients
who shared their lives with me and who
showed me the strength of the human spirit.*

and

*To the memory of my father, Victor, who shared his
boundless love of learning with me; to my loving mother,
Harriet; and to my husband, Lloyd, and my son, Adam.*
RHG

*To my parents, who told me I could go anywhere I wanted in life,
and then helped me get there.*
CEH

CONTENTS

PREFACE

OWNSIZING, RIGHTSIZING, RESTRUCTURING, RE-ENGINEERING —whatever you call it, it usually means that people are going to lose their jobs. Many workers and their families will find themselves in a world they have not prepared for. Some people will have to leave the only company they ever worked for.

The ongoing reorganization of American business has affected how we think of our jobs and our careers, no matter how much experience we have. In recent years, thousands of workers lost their jobs just as they reached the height of their careers, and many younger people today are frustrated by frequent job changes as they try to launch the careers they've chosen.

This book on surviving in the constantly changing business environment is among the first to provide a practical and focused approach to issues confronting the American work force. As Americans are forced to change their expectations, the authors suggest a way for redefining one's career goals and making them fit within a larger plan for personal success and happiness. *Climb a Fallen Ladder* deals sensibly and sensitively with the attitudes, skills, and characteristics needed to thrive personally and professionally.

The qualities that brought career success in the past are no longer the keys to the future. Traditional bureaucratic skills emphasized an inward-looking career perspective, one that suited experts in specialized areas. The new workplace demands an external perspective, one focused on customers and financial results. Employees today must be generalists, with skills that are adaptable as business conditions and priorities shift. Companies are hiring and retaining workers who demonstrate versatility and the ability to learn quickly.

While they seek to improve their national as well as international competitiveness, American companies are becoming flatter and expect all employees to perform roles that cross over traditional departmental boundaries. In essence, there are fewer ladders to climb—and more bridges to cross.

With willingness and courage, the authors argue, anybody can find and develop these skills within his or her learning experience. Learning does not have an age limit. A 50-year-old manager can be as adaptable, flexible, and creative as a person half that age—and by demonstrating those abilities, he or she can be just as valuable in the new business environment.

We are experiencing an economic change as profound as the one accompanying the Industrial Revolution. The heroes of that revolution had the patience to overcome obstacles stretching over years. They looked to the future, not the past, to define and redefine their measures of success. Stephenson spent 15 years to perfect the locomotive. Watts worked for 30 years on the condensing engine. Hard rubber cost Goodyear 10 years of poverty and public ridicule. Railroad executives treated Westinghouse as a lunatic and scoffed at his idea for "stopping a train by wind" before he was finally able to sell the air brake.

Most of us respond in a predictable way to the rocks in our path. We complain and we kick them—and only hurt ourselves. But we can use the obstacles in life—including job losses and career changes —as stepping stones on our own personal paths to success. I'm confident this book will help show you how.

–RON P. SIMMONS
Chief Operating Officer, DVC, Inc.
and author of *Value Directed Management*

TO THE READER

MORE THAN 20 YEARS have passed since I finished my residency in psychiatry at Mount Sinai Medical Center in New York City. During that time, in my private practice, I've spent literally tens of thousands of hours in deep conversation with people from all walks of life. I've been listening—trying to hear what people are saying about themselves even when they're talking about something else; observing their reactions even when they don't know they're reacting; connecting events and emotions that, once connected, can help them understand why they feel and act the way they do. And most of all, I've been guiding them to new levels of feeling, thought, and behavior.

Traditionally, psychiatry has been a solitary endeavor accomplished one person at a time. In fact, this is the psychiatrist's strength: to go as far into your thoughts and feelings as you'll allow, untangle your webs of anxiety and anger, and help set you on a relatively smooth road. This process is an intensely personal matter, different for each individual. A psychiatrist specializes in helping each person make the most of an individual life.

Even so, I think we've entered a time in our nation's history when many Americans are experiencing similar feelings, needing to hear similar words. Collectively, we need to reach new conclusions about our work and new relationships with our employers. I've come to this belief largely because of what I've observed in my own practice.

As with most psychiatrists during the 1970s and '80s, most of my patients came to me with relational problems, personal problems, family problems. We would collaborate, the patient and I, in an effort to understand those problems, why they came to be, and how to create new ways of responding to them. Only occasionally was the patient's job the primary issue.

But sometime in late 1989 or early 1990, I began to notice a change. A new patient came to my office whose anxiety problems stemmed largely from her work—by itself, not a terribly noteworthy event. Shortly thereafter, however, another new patient brought a similar complaint. Within months, a third and then a fourth and then a fifth new patient came to see me about emotional problems tied directly to work. At the same time, incredibly, it seemed that many of my existing patients began talking more openly and more urgently about the anxieties and affronts they were suffering on the job.

They told me that work problems were acutely affecting their relationships, their sleep, their outlook on life, and their thoughts about themselves. In years past, that influence usually flowed in the opposite direction.

The shift started imperceptibly, as a small eddy in a wide stream. But soon it became an unstoppable tide that altered the lives of my patients and the emphasis of my practice. I wondered what in the world was happening. Was this just a remarkable coincidence, or was my practice a microcosm of a much larger wave of change rolling through the American workplace?

It wasn't long before the media began to answer that question for me. Nowadays, everyone seems to be talking about downsizing, rightsizing, reorganizing, re-engineering—any one of the growing list of words used to describe what's happening in the American workplace. We talk about which layoff was announced last week, about how many jobs will vaporize, about the typically jubilant reaction of the stock market, about the size of the CEO's bonus.

But in the midst of it all, no one seems to be addressing the feelings of workers—the people hardest hit by the news; the people who have to live and work in the aftermath of the tidal wave. It's as though society is standing helplessly by, saying, "We don't know how to solve your problem, so we simply won't talk about it."

I think we have to talk about it. Anxiety created by rapid and relentless corporate change will likely become the defining mental health issue of our time. Many of us have become dissatisfied with our jobs yet terrified that we might lose them. We're laboring harder than ever—at work and at home—but we don't feel the pleasure of getting ahead. We're trying desperately to cope with rapid-fire changes even as they shatter our basic assumptions about employment and its unspoken promises. No doubt about it. It's a tough time to be an American worker.

But now I have to say something that, at first, may seem surprising. As terrifying and traumatic as this time may feel to many of us, I believe it could lead to something very positive. Why? Because virtually every crisis contains embedded opportunities. This one is no exception. It will allow us—force us, perhaps—to take a new look at ourselves, to reevaluate the meaning and importance of work in our lives, to shake off our inertia and get moving again in a new and better direction.

What I've seen in my patients has led me to a profound belief in human strength and resilience. I'm convinced that, with willingness and work, you can meet the challenge this crisis brings. And by doing so, you'll prove to yourself once again that you are adaptable and strong. You'll find that you have a great potential to master new skills, new concepts, and new ways of viewing the world, and that you can take charge of your life at a time when many people feel less in charge than ever. You can use this crisis to build personal strengths you never thought possible. I hope this book will help.

Don't get me wrong. There's still a complex and intensely personal journey ahead of you, ahead of us all. The going may be rough.

For many of us, it already is. But remember that thinking in new ways can open new doors. And the journey into yourself can bring rewards beyond imagining. As you read the concepts presented in these pages, take whatever amount of time you need to digest and personalize thoughts that I can describe in only general ways. Don't forget that there are no pat answers, no quick fixes. As I tell my patients, when it comes to adopting new ways of thought, you have to work it through—a process that requires time, motivation, and the courage to change. By finding that courage in the face of fear, you'll prove to yourself once again that you have what it takes to meet life's challenges, now and in the years to come.

Rochelle H. Gordon, M.D.

PART I

The Working Worried

I

Caught in a Riptide

IKNEW JACK WELL. Well enough, anyway, to know that he had a hot temper, and that he was just starting to burn. I'd seen it many times over many years, this sudden flash of anger blasting out of him, scorching anything in its path. I had to admit, though, that this time was a little different. Usually quick to burn himself out, this time Jack couldn't seem to stop. He went on for nearly 30 minutes, ranting and raving about his employer. He recounted one indignity after another, gaining speed and fury as he went. Eventually he slowed and finally stopped, heaved a dejected sigh, and whispered, almost to himself, "I never liked that job anyway"—a statement I knew was untrue.

Looking at him, I wondered how much of his story *was* true, how much exaggerated, and how much fabricated. Could his boss have held secret department meetings, openly excluding Jack and two other doomed employees from the annual planning sessions? Could the personnel manager have handed Jack a pink slip without warning or apology, right there in his cubicle, then stood watch while he packed up his desk? Could the company have allowed the regional

director to fire a "lifer" just 18 months before his pension kicked in?
I was a little skeptical.

A few days later I made a lunch date with a friend who happened
to be a vice president at a large but shrinking corporation. I asked for
his observations about corporate policies and an explanation of
downsizing as he knew it. After he finished, I asked if events like
those Jack described could happen. He said, "Sure, that's exactly what
happens." I was shocked. But that was 1989, before I knew what I
know now.

The Real Thing

When you're trying to untangle an emotional issue, it's helpful to
know how that issue fits into the culture that surrounds it. That's why
I asked my corporate friend about the incidents Jack recounted to me.
That's also why I started tracking the evolution of corporate culture
through the early 1990s. My patients were describing more and more
of their feelings about it: the anxiety, the anger, the sense of powerlessness and failure. By and large, these were intelligent, hard-
working people, not people who should have been afraid of losing
their jobs. Or so I thought, until I started learning more about corporate reorganizing and downsizing. I read everything I could find on
the topic. Eventually, it ballooned to hundreds of books and articles.
I talked at length with people who created corporate policies, and
with people who opposed them. And I began to gain my own perspective on my patients' feelings and fears.

Of course, I am not an economist, and this book is not about the
American economy. What you'll find here are tools and perspectives
to help you live with courage and optimism in this age of rapid
change and instability. But first we need to make a brief stop at the
source of the crisis, in the analytical, fact-based world of business. Because *this* fact can't be denied: Corporate policies in America today
have profoundly influenced mental health in America today. By getting to the source of our anxiety—and understanding it—we're more
likely to find the shortest road to feeling better about it.

If you shovel all my reading and research into one massive pot, I think it all boils down to two basic statements. First, American workers have plenty of reasons to be anxious. And second, what's happening is no one's fault. Sounds simple, doesn't it? But in my opinion, these two statements provide keys to unlock the emotional maze that traps us in work-related anger and anxiety. And they provide our starting point for the personal journey ahead.

A Pretty Picture

On the surface, the American economy looks pretty good these days. In fact, it has for a number of years. By year-end 1995, overall unemployment had declined to about 5.6 percent. Unemployment levels for *managers* had plummeted to 2.4 percent. Inflation hovered at just 2.5 percent. Corporations averaged double-digit profits for the third year in a row. The stock market had risen nearly 40 percent, hitting more than 80 record highs along the way. The federal deficit even fell. A picture of idyllic life in America, right? But if that's true, then how do you explain the other side of the picture?

On the flip side, it seems that nearly everyone is nervous. This time of stable economy and strong corporate profits turns out to be a time of anxiety for literally millions of American workers. Studies say that one in three worry about a family member losing a job in the next year. And a vast sea of people—some 100 million—aren't sure their income will exceed their expenses. There seems to be a big hole in the rosy economic picture where middle-class American workers used to sit.

Why is that? Lots of people have told me it's because of the downsizing, of course. After all, the people who count these things say that more than 40 million jobs disappeared between 1973 and 1995. Nearly a half-million jobs vanished in 1995 alone, plus almost 200,000 more in the first quarter of 1996. That's a lot of jobs. But despite these big numbers and the fears they create, I don't think this loss of jobs is the real crux of our problem. There are more jobs available in America than ever. And at least one large study claims that

The Language of Layoffs

Layoffs have become so widespread that a whole language has risen up to describe the phenomenon, most of it coined to avoid using real words like "fired" and "unemployed." Downsizing is still the term most commonly used. Here are some of the others.

Career change opportunity
Career transition program
Coerced transition
Decruiting
Deployment
Destaffing
Elimination of employment security policy
Focused reduction
Force management
Involuntary separation from payroll
Involuntary severance
Not going forward
Payroll adjustment
Personnel surplus reduction
Redeployment
Redundancy elimination
Repositioning
Reshaping
Resource release
Riffed (from reduction in force, or RIF)
Rightsizing
Schedule adjustment
Severed
Skill mix adjustment
Strengthening global security
Unassignment
Work force adjustment
Work force imbalance correction

people aren't leaving jobs any more rapidly than they ever have. The real problem, from an emotional point of view, is that a larger number of people are leaving their jobs by *force* than by choice. They're getting laid off. And in today's lingo, laid off means fired. Unlike the good old days, there's no return to the assembly line, no callback when business surges once again. Companies are making fundamental changes in the way they do business—and deep cuts in the staff they do it with, especially white-collar workers.

So, more people than ever are getting laid off as businesses scramble to be players on the world stage. This would probably be enough to make us feel vulnerable and out of control. But here's the crowning blow. Remember the net increase in jobs I mentioned earlier? It's true that American business has created more jobs than it's destroyed. But many of the new jobs offer less pay and lower prestige than the jobs that are disappearing. Many are part-time and lack benefits. In fact, reports say that a supplier of temporary workers has become America's largest employer.

This leaves two issues to worry over: the possibility of losing a job you're not ready to leave, and the possibility of not finding as good a job to replace it if you do. In this day and age, these are both distinct possibilities. And they lie at the root of our nervousness.

The lopsided gains of the already-rich only add anger to the anxiety. You've probably heard people say that the rich in America are getting richer and the poor are getting poorer. The latest statistics bear this out. In 1994, for example, 10 percent of American households controlled nearly 70 percent of the nation's wealth. Add to that the increasing disparity between what the CEO takes home and what an average worker takes home. It used to be, 20 years ago or so, that the CEO earned roughly 40 times more than an average worker. In round numbers, if the average worker earned $25,000 a year, for example, the average CEO probably made a million. Sounds like a lot, doesn't it? Well these days, if the average worker earns $25,000 a year, the average CEO probably makes $4 to 5 million.

Maybe if we were all getting ahead together, this disparity would go down easier. But we're not. The average American CEO's income jumped something like 20 percent in 1995 alone. In contrast, the average American worker's income has backwatered. After figuring for inflation, economists say family income is the same today as it was 20 years ago. And because so many families now need two wage-earners to stay afloat, we are, in fact, slowly sinking.

In a nutshell, these are the abundant—and very real—reasons why we're nervous. They're why a growing number of us are a little cynical, struggling to stay motivated, unwilling to become personally invested in company business, unhappy about working more hours than we want to, afraid of what the future holds.

No One to Blame

Why is all this happening, and whom can we blame for it? I've heard more than one patient conclude that the CEO and top executives must be whiling away their ivory-tower time dreaming up ways to stick it to the workers. But, really, while the anger is understandable, this idea is absurd. It's simply the easiest thing to say when you don't have a better explanation. And there are a number of better explanations.

One big reason for the current corporate chaos is that, while our economy is steady, it isn't especially strong. Economists say that, for 100 years before 1973, America had a long-term growth rate of something over 3 percent. Over the next 20 years, however, from 1973 to 1993, that growth rate fell to something over 2 percent. Those numbers seem pretty small, almost inconsequential really. But they aren't. That's because the difference between growing at a 2 percent rate and growing at a 3 percent rate is not 1 percent; it's 50 percent. Can you see it? An economy growing at a 2 percent rate would have to increase by half to reach 3 percent. If we had continued at our 3 percent historical rate, we would have been some $12 trillion ahead of where we ended up in 1993. We'd be even farther ahead now. To make matters worse, most experts expect our growth rate to stay in its current vicinity well past the year 2000.

The short message here is that America is not as far ahead as it used to be. That leads me to the second big reason for corporate chaos: global competition. The rest of the world is catching up, and fast. Exploding technology and a global marketplace mean you can do business for a third, a tenth, a hundredth of what it used to cost on American soil, whether you're making computers, clothes, or almost anything else. Foreign companies are making products to compete with ours, in both price and quality. And American companies are expanding overseas to stay competitive at home. This is no one's fault. It's just the way business works.

These worldwide forces are unlike anything we've experienced before. In the 1960s, one or two companies out of 10 faced competition offshore. Now the number is more like eight out of 10. We're not talking only about product competition here. We're talking about *job* competition. About the growing number of people from other countries who are rapidly gaining skills and technology in lands where the standard of living is still way below ours. They can do your job well, for less, and be happy for the work. If you were the company president, would you ignore them?

Companies are also clamping down at home to squeeze the most profit pennies out of every dollar and, hopefully, to compete better against cheaper labor. To the employees, however, sometimes the clamps feel too tight. For example, one large communications company barred operators from saying "thank you" to customers because it took too much time. Another company's employee manual demands that long-distance calls made with a company phone card be reimbursed by the widow if an employee dies. Much more common than these affronts is the burgeoning "Big Brother" tracking of personal productivity. Cash registers grade their operators' accuracy. Computers count the speed of the fingers on their keyboards. Internal e-mail messages, which many employees believe to be private, are routinely screened by company moles. All of this in an effort to goad employees into working harder and longer, at a higher level of productivity than ever.

Another big factor fueling corporate evolution is the stock market, which blesses and curses public companies based primarily on the balance sheet. Since downsizing typically makes a short-term improvement in the bottom line, the market has rewarded the trend. When AT&T announced 40,000 layoffs, the stock spiked by $2.75 a share. Sears planned to cut 50,000 and the stock rose by almost 4 percent. Xerox promised to clip 10,000 jobs and its stock responded by 7 percent.

People are in the stock market to make money, after all. And for a long time now, the stock market has been the best place to make it. Since 1980, the Standard & Poor's 500 has bestowed more than a 15 percent return on investment. If you have a pension plan, a 401(k) plan, or a nest egg invested for the future, you are probably one of those people reaping benefits from a strong market. If your job is threatened, you may be one of those people corporations are shifting around in an effort to drive that stock price higher. This effort may be good for the country's investors (including you). It may be good for the bottom line (also including you, if your company has a profit-sharing plan). If you're one of those people who loses a job, however, it certainly won't feel good to you. But you can't blame a business for trying to be successful; that's what business is about.

Of course, you can't blame yourself either. It's not your fault that business is changing at such a rapid rate. It's not your fault that companies have settled on downsizing as a way to get ahead. It's not your fault that technology is mushrooming or that competition is breathing down your neck. Was it the blacksmith's fault that cars were invented? No. Was it the watchmaker's fault that quartz timing became the rage? Of course not. You are living and working just as Americans have for the past 50 years, but the environment around you is in a revolutionary change. Sometimes it feels like a rowboat headed for Niagara Falls.

Hopefully, you can see by now that there's really nothing and no one to blame except the march of history. Keep in mind that, to many corporate leaders, the choice is not between progress and status quo. The choice is between progress and corporate death. Is downsizing the best way to make progress? I suppose only history can judge that. In the meantime, whether you lose your job or keep it, you are still responsible for your own life, and still the only one who can find your path through the maze. Blaming the environment around you is understandable, but it will not show you the way.

We all know that there are good guys and bad guys in the world. But that's not what this corporate revolution is about. This is a much more complex issue—and a much less personal one. Hundreds of thousands of people are being laid off. This is not about unfeeling, in-humane CEOs. We're all just people, trying to do the best we can within our own priorities. We're all subject to the same centrifugal force that seems so strong just now. We're all trying to find the best way through it.

A Turning Point

Many factors have combined to bring us to this turning point in American history, a point probably not unlike the Industrial Revo-lution. This is a period of massive change, and we don't know where we're going. All we know is that, right now, everything seems to be shifting under our feet, morphing before we're ready. And change plus velocity is a high-speed road to anxiety. This is especially true for those of us old enough to have grown up at a time when we expected employment to be permanent—when we sought a predictable life with a guaranteed income. And for many of us, for a while, it seemed to be working.

It's natural to fear the end of what seemed like a predictable and stable life. You'd be crazy not to. The whole texture of our society is changing. A way of life that we took for granted is fading away. We have to adjust to the fact that employers no longer want to be our parents; they want to be our associates, our clients. We have to handle the company's demand that we work longer and harder, with a smaller staff. We have to absorb and process information at a more rapid rate than we've ever known, using equipment we may never have imagined. We have to learn that success in today's business world is tied almost totally to how much we produce. We have to accept that middle age is no longer a time to coast through our working lives.

This is bound to bring up some emotions. We've had an economic earthquake that's shattering our ideas about the nature of work, the rewards of work, indeed, our very identities. The edifice we've been building since the end of World War II seems to be falling around us. But keep in mind that people are displaced and deposed in every revolution. The Industrial Revolution seemed like a very dark time. But it created unheralded opportunities for the future. In the Great Depression, people thought they'd never work again. Then, too, many opportunities were spawned from adversity. In an editorial written for *Newsweek* magazine, AT&T's chief, Robert E. Allen, said about our revolution that companies don't have room for all of yesterday's jobs, but they *will* create the jobs of tomorrow. Is he correct? Time will surely tell us.

Historically, only during this brief time since World War II has life seemed so predictable. The idea of someone providing for us, taking care of us—whether it be Medicare, Social Security, or an employer—has had a very short tenure. Even so, the prospect of that safety net failing gives us plenty of reasons to be nervous.

What Now?

So it seems that Jack was telling the truth. This is not your imagination. Anxiety walks the hallways freely in most of America's large corporations and even in many mom-and-pop shops. It lounges by the water coolers and glides through the executive suite in expensive shoes. It has no favorites. It relies on change and fear to maintain its strength. A colleague laughing in the boss's office: *Will he be the one they keep?* A meeting to which you were not invited: *Will they hang me out to dry?* A project given to a junior staffer: *Will my higher salary endanger my future?*

It's human nature to worry over these things. After all, we have families to raise and bills to pay and jobs with which we identify. Our emotions are understandable, perfectly normal to some degree. But just for a moment, consider another point of view, a new possibility more in keeping with your health and well-being.

Consider this: How much good does it do you to be upset and anxious? How much good does it do you to blame your employer, or corporate America in general, for your problems or potential problems? Frankly, the short answer to both questions is, "None." It does you no good. It may seem justified from your perspective. It may be what everyone else is doing. It may be the easiest thing to talk about around the lunch table. But going down this path is a sure journey to an unhappy future. Don't do it. Don't take the easy road to the bitter end.

Let's take a good hard look at this. What *are* you accomplishing if you're angry, defeated, full of blame and invective? Only one thing, as far as I can tell. You're wasting your time. And time is the most important asset you have. Would you stand on a balcony heaving money into the street to show your displeasure with corporate America? Of course not. So let's be very clear about this. Flinging your time into the abyss is doing the same thing, if not worse.

You can't stop what's happening in corporate America, and there's no one to blame for it. So take the bull by the horns. Take the challenge of the future, in your own mind and in your own way. Once you make that decision, you've made a U-turn onto the road that leads to personal fulfillment. The real question is, "What now?"

From a mental health perspective, there are a number of things you can do now. The chapters that follow will introduce you to tools and concepts you can use to feel freer and happier, more aware of what's important to you, and less willing to translate job insecurity into personal insecurity. You'll learn to be less afraid of the future while, at the same time, taking more control of your life in the present. You'll discover ways to define your personal priorities—and ways to keep your working life in line with them. You'll embrace new skill-building techniques to make yourself more valuable to an employer while making yourself stronger on your own. You'll find out how attitudes and expectations affect your response to job loss, and how you can mold them into spirit-building coping skills. And you'll realize that new perspectives and ways of communicating can help build your circle of significant others into a powerful, supportive team. Are you ready?

2

Releasing Control

O NCE UPON A TIME, when those of us sprouting our first gray hairs were little children, the world seemed like a predictable place. We played. We went to school. We grew up and fell in love. We knew that, if we worked hard, we'd get ahead. This was the American promise in the land of opportunity. And the promise felt so good, so stable. We loved the feeling of being in control. No surprises. No changes without our permission. Everything proceeding according to plan, except, of course, for the spontaneous long weekend taken here and there, at carefully spaced intervals. A steady income with regular raises formed the foundation of this very good life.

Certainly, Steve Waterman had little reason to doubt this picture for himself. In his mid-40s, Steve had been married 14 years to his best friend and biggest love. Two years after the wedding, the happy couple moved to southern California, where Steve went to work for a large industrial company known for the dedication of its lifelong employees. He liked his job and, more important, he was on a steady career path—good money, promotions every couple of years. By the time his children were ages 6 months, 8, and 10, Steve had become a middle manager. He supervised a division of 350 hard-working people looking for the same kind of life Steve had. He got along well with his staff, even the guys on the line, joking with them and occasionally eating lunch with them in the "mess," as they called it. He never told them so, but Steve believed that his management position meant he should work more hours than the other guys. So after the shift went home, Steve usually stayed on a while, making sure everything was in order and thinking up ways to increase quality and speed. Everything felt predictable, pleasant.

One sunny California day when the midwest was shrouded in snow, the chief operations officer—the boss's boss—appeared at Steve's door unannounced to talk with him. A too-tall, too-thin man, he folded himself solemnly into the chair across from Steve's desk. Steve could feel his heart beating under the knot in his tie.

"Steve," the executive started matter-of-factly, "you've done a great job for us here at the plant. So I want you to think about something. Our midwest facility is still struggling to deal with last year's increase in the price of raw materials. I'd like you to go out there and see what you can do about it. Cut costs a few points, raise production a bit. Probably take you about six months to get it turned around. I know that's a long time to be away from your family, but you can come home every other weekend. And it'll be good for your future with the company. We'll take care of things here for you while you're gone. I know you'll want to talk this over with your wife before you make a decision, but I'm sure you'll do the right thing."

Before Steve could collect his thoughts, the man was gone. Elated by the compliment, Steve was also dismayed. Six months? His baby daughter Emily would be a different person in six months. Matthew's Little League season would be over. Steve would be unprepared for the Sunday school program he had to teach. What would his wife think? Even as this question crossed Steve's mind, he knew it didn't matter. They asked him to go. He had to go. He went.

A Fragile Security

Steve came to my office about eight weeks after returning from his midwest assignment, which lasted eight months and didn't work out quite as well as he had hoped. Several days after he got home, Steve told me, he'd awakened at about four in the morning with his heart racing, unable to catch his breath, afraid he was having a heart attack. The whole family went to the emergency room with him. Doctors there checked him over, ran an electrocardiogram, did some blood work, and found nothing. They sent him home and told him to come back if it happened again. Over the next five weeks, it did happen again—twice. But doctors still couldn't find anything wrong. They started calling the episodes panic attacks, Steve said, barely hiding his disgust at the thought, and they suggested that he talk with someone about them. I asked Steve if he knew of anything that was troubling him.

"Well, yes, actually," he said with a one-shouldered shrug, "but I don't think it has anything to do with this." It turns out that Sam, Steve's friend and mentor, had been ushered out the front door of the plant the Friday before Steve's return to work. On Monday, Steve found Sam's office dark and obviously vacant, his name and title already scraped from the glass beside the office door. I suggested that that experience was enough to upset almost anyone. But Steve said, "No, Sam is one of the best. People know him all over the industry. It's really strange that he's gone. But I know he'll find another job. And we'll get along okay at the plant without him."

We sat quietly for a moment while Steve looked down at his hands. Then I asked, "Do you know why Sam was fired?" Steve's head snapped up and I saw his puzzled, distinctly frightened eyes. He said, "No, I don't have any idea. Twenty-eight other people were let go on the same day. Sam's boss told us some story about new business directions, but we still don't know exactly what that means."

So here was the issue. If Sam—a leader in the industry—could

What Is a Panic Attack?

A panic attack involves at least four of these symptoms:

- trouble catching your breath, or the feeling that you're smothering
- feeling dizzy, unsteady, or faint
- palpitations or a racing heart
- trembling or shaking
- sweating
- choking
- nausea or stomach upset
- feeling that you aren't real, or your environment isn't
- numbness or tingling
- feeling flushed or chilled
- discomfort or pain in your chest
- fear that you're dying
- fear that you're going crazy or will do something uncontrolled

Panic attacks occur unexpectedly, at a time when you're not otherwise anxious or the focus of other people's attention. And, by definition, panic attacks can't have a physical cause, such as an excessive caffeine intake, a reaction to drugs, or an overactive thyroid. As in Steve's case, good medical care—both physical and emotional—can help to identify the cause of panic attacks and resolve it.

lose his job that easily, maybe Steve could too. And even though Steve hadn't said it to himself out loud, his mind was grappling with that very thought in the middle of the night. He'd already strained his family with a long absence. His children were in expensive private schools. The second car would need to be replaced soon. His wife wanted a new house so the kids could have separate rooms. But after what happened to Sam, Steve's pleasant, solid future now seemed studded with land mines. After all that had happened, he couldn't possibly tell his wife more bad news about work. So alone in his dreams at night, Steve wrestled with the fear that life was slipping out of his control.

Living the Illusion

Like most of us, Steve had worked hard to construct a life that seemed constant and predictable. He knew what to expect each day, and he'd come to relish the feeling of being the master of his destiny, provider for his family. But the reality is that Steve never did have control over his life. None of us do. Life is not predictable, and we can't choose the events that come our way. The feeling of control that we work so hard to maintain is just an illusion we build to keep from constantly worrying about what disaster might be coming around the next bend. Despite our best efforts to create a picture of predictability, the fact is that we are not in charge.

There are only two sure things in life: You were born, and you will die. That's it. You really don't know what's going to happen to you a minute, an hour, a day, a week from now. Consider the 26-year-old school teacher walking to work on a crowded street in New York City. An air conditioner fell from a window high above and hit her on the head. Of all the things she spent her time trying to keep under control, do you think she ever worried about *that* possibility? Or consider my friend's father, hit by a driver who zoomed onto the freeway using an exit ramp. These things happen. You can't control them. Of course, it's not just bad things that are outside our control.

Someone wins the lottery almost every day of the week. Or what about the adopted dog who saves a family from their burning house by barking loudly enough to wake them up?

We think of these events as lightning bolts, as strokes of incredibly bad or good luck. But what is luck, after all? It's simply a word for describing the odd occurrences that feel like they're outside our control. We've lived in an era when it was possible to maintain the illusion that, except for these occasional bolts from the blue, economic life has been pretty much under control.

For much of the time since World War II, America has been on a steady climb. During this segment of our history—a breathlessly short bit of time by any standard of measurement—workers seemed to do better and better, and children routinely had more than their parents. No one promised us that this trend would continue. But because it was all we knew, we came to think of it as normal, expected. A change for the worse seemed wrong, somehow. A change for the better was, well, expected. Prosperity seemed so normal, in fact, that we constructed safety nets to erase any thought that the future could be threatened or wrestled out of our control. We invented Medicare, Medicaid, Social Security, pension plans provided by employers. Just outside the bounds of our lifetimes, these things did not exist. When you got old, your children took care of you. If you didn't have children, you figured out another way. But in the time of America's 20th-century growth spurt, we thought we could control not only the present but the future too.

The point I'm getting to here is that the things we've taken for granted about life and work, as if they were carved in stone like the Ten Commandments, were never sure things. Job security was never a promise, never a guarantee. And the longer we hold onto this myth, the longer we will prevent ourselves from accepting reality, embracing unpredictability, and finding our own resilience in the face of change.

It's understandable that we have come to rely on the predictability of life. Think of it this way: Just like everyone else, you have formed thoughts and conclusions about life and the people around you based largely on what you learned from the family you grew up in. This may not be a conscious process. You may not realize you're doing it. But you are. It's because what you grew up with is all you knew. Likewise, we as a country have based our thoughts and conclusions about work on this particular moment in history. It's all we've known. It's completely understandable that we should do this. But it has lulled us into being resistant to the unpredictable and resentful for having to deal with it.

A scientist would say that we've based our conclusion on a single small sample—a dangerous thing to do because the conclusion could easily be wrong. In statistics, you have to be sure you study a sample big enough to accurately represent the variety in the whole population you want to know something about. That's why, when you see opinion polls on the evening news, they tell you how many people they interviewed. It gives you a better idea of how accurate the results are. If they interviewed two people, you could rightly think, "Well, that was just the opinion of two people. They don't represent the whole." If they interviewed two thousand, on the other hand, those results are hard to ignore. Chances are their opinions will indeed reflect the opinions of the group as a whole. So if you are 35 years old, the sample on which you're basing your expectation of life is just 35 years out of the thousands of years of recorded history. That's a very small sample in a rapidly changing world. Throughout history, we've evolved through major societal changes, many of which involved misery and suffering of the sort that virtually none of us have ever known. We happened to be born in the right place at the right time. So we developed a set of expectations about what life should look like and how the world should treat us based on this tiny little sample of time. This is natural. It's all we've known. But it also sets us up for anxiety and discontent when we meet the unexpected.

Free from Fear

Once you come to understand and accept that we are not in control of what happens to us, you've opened yourself to a fascinating and healthy change of attitude. You stop worrying so much about it. You find yourself becoming less rigid. You begin to look at life in a more global way, accepting what comes instead of struggling to stay in control. One of the biggest problems with living under the illusion of control is that sometimes we hold on so tight to our picture of what life should be like that we miss opportunities. Because as often as not, those opportunities come in a package stamped CRISIS ENCLOSED.

One of the keys to releasing control successfully is in your attitude, your mental focus. In general, people have a tendency to see what they're looking for. It's called a mental set. Here's an example. If two people are out walking together, one looking for birds and the other looking for wildflowers, chances are that they'll each see more of what they personally set out to find. The birder will probably miss some of the wildflowers, and the botanist will probably miss some of the birds. Primarily, they'll see what they're focused on seeing. So by looking for positive outcomes and exciting opportunities even in moments of crisis, you'll probably increase your chances of finding them. By focusing on unfairness and disaster, you'll probably increase your chances of finding that.

This is, in a general way, what it means to be an optimist. It's important to be an optimist—first, to have confidence that things will work out, and second, to have confidence in your ability to make it through if something doesn't work out. This, to me, is the height of mental health. How do you become an optimist? Start by looking at your life and thinking about all the hard things you've come through. Nine out of 10 of the people I talk with can look back and say they've made it through a number of difficult things in life. If you can say that too, you have tremendous resources on which to build an optimistic attitude.

No one ever wishes for a crisis, but you're bound to get a few. No life escapes adversity. Remember that old make-lemons-into-lemonade advice from the '70s? It's pretty sound advice from a mental health perspective. Or, as an equestrian friend of mine is fond of saying, "When you step in a pile of manure, there's bound to be a pony somewhere nearby." So when what's happening around you seems messy and out of control, you better start looking for that pony.

Steps to Acceptance

In general, the knowledge that you could be laid off at any moment makes for an inefficient, anxiety-plagued workforce. It's analogous to living in London during the blitz. You are not going to sit quietly at your desk, concentrating fully on your work. You're going to be nervous and scared about when the next big bomb is going to fall, and where it's going to hit. If you *are* laid off, especially after 10, 15, 20 years with the same company, it's going to rock your feelings of security and control over your life. When you get another job and they expect you to do half again as much work for 25 percent less pay, it feels even worse. There's no getting around the fact that events like these can make you feel as though your foundation is cracking.

But this new knowledge that your employer can separate you from your job isn't really anything new. It's just that we can see it now. Employers are exercising that power more now, but they've always had it. Keep in mind that it's much better to see things for what they are than to go on living in an illusion of control. It's much better to be able to identify the forces affecting you, so you can address them directly rather than being surprised by them later.

By embracing the unpredictability of employment, you can help reduce your anxiety level about it. This may seem hard, but look at it this way. Whatever is going to happen is going to happen, whether you worry about it or not. If you spend your time and energy worrying about what's going to happen, you're engaging in something called anticipatory anxiety. You're anxious about something that hasn't happened yet—something that may not happen at all. If you spend too much time worrying about it, or your anxiety level gets too high, it robs your energy and takes your mind off what you can be doing *now* to set yourself up for success when the next crisis comes along.

One of the main reasons why people don't want to embrace the unpredictability of employment is that coming to this conclusion requires a response. It requires some initiative on your part to prepare yourself, to look around you and be willing to see what's happening. This is no time to stick your head in the sand and pretend everything's okay. Maybe the time will come when jobs are once again more secure than they are today. But for now, we are in a state of flux. So if you want to survive what's happening in America today, you have to accept the fact that there is no such thing as job security. You have no choice.

Picture it this way. Imagine you're in a canoe going happily down the uncharted river of life. You've been sliding along for days or weeks on clean, flat water when suddenly you hit rapids. Maybe you had warning of turbulence. Maybe you didn't. But now you have a choice. You can become terrified and stop paddling because no one told you there would be rapids on this trip. (Did anyone tell you there wouldn't be?) Or you can paddle harder and find the best way through it. If you choose the former reaction, the river will consume you. If you choose the latter, you may get battered, but you'll get through. Do you really have a choice here?

If you can embrace the unpredictable nature of life, prepare as best you can for the unknown, and become optimistic that things will work out, life becomes less burdened. The worries that threatened to overwhelm you about the unknown disaster around the bend seem to fade in their intensity. The more you hold onto control, the more you face the impossible task of protecting yourself from any change or crisis. The less you hold onto control, the more free you are to adjust to changes and crises, and to find the good things in them. You can learn to find the opportunities embedded in every crisis; you can even learn to welcome the changes those opportunities bring. Since change is the only real constant in life, walking yourself through this process of releasing control may be the best gift you can give yourself. Try meditation. Or, if you're religious, try adopting the philosophy, "Let go and let God." Whatever method works best for you, use it to give yourself that gift of releasing control.

These days, even Steve has begun to call it a gift. Although Steve is still working for the same big industrial company, he thinks about it differently now. He doesn't rely on that company for his lifetime employment. He's putting money aside to live on in case his job disappears. He thinks about the big picture more often—how his industry fits into America's business direction, and how his company stacks up against its competitors. He's more interested in what the other companies in his field are doing, who's coming and going, what products are in development, what possibilities exist for *him*. He even installed a contact manager on his computer so he can keep in touch with colleagues in the industry. Interestingly enough, this personal evolution has reaped an extra benefit. Besides making Steve feel less anxious about his future, his professional development has made Steve an even more valuable partner in his employer's business.

3

Who's in Charge Here?

OFTEN, when I talk with people about the idea of releasing control, they struggle. They resist. The more motivated and capable the person, the deeper the heels drag in the dirt. I can almost hear the silent self-conversation. "Does she want me to just give up? Let go? I couldn't possibly. What would happen to my children, my job, my responsibilities? I'm trying to be successful here!"

And you know what? That reaction is right. You have to release control, but you can't ever stop taking control. This sounds completely contradictory, doesn't it? How can these two statements both be true? Well, they are. They're both true because, as with many things in life, the concept of control has two elements that work best in balance. When I suggest that you try to release control, I'm talking about letting go of the things you never really had control over in the first place—the unmanageable things you were trying desperately to manage, the capricious things you hoped anxiety and worry could magically influence. I'm not suggesting that you become a noodle in a pot of boiling water, a feather in whatever gale comes along. I'm suggesting that you stop trying to control the uncontrollable.

But you can't accomplish this in the most healthy way until you adopt the counterbalance to it as well. As important as it is for you to relinquish control of the uncontrollable, it's equally as important that you *take* control of the rest. Oddly enough, sometimes we labor so hard over things we can't control, that what we can and should control slides by unnoticed until it's too late. With the current corporate turbulence, this mistake could be more costly than ever. If you can find a way to take charge of the parts of life you can and should control, you'll probably avoid what happened to Louise Kincaid.

A Different Drummer

Tall and slender, in her mid–40s, Louise Kincaid appeared in my office for her first appointment wearing black cigarette-leg Levi's, black ostrich skin boots, and a black silk tank top. A long mane of black hair hung in a thick bush down her back, streaked with a few strands of silver and constrained only by one big barrette swinging just below shoulder level—not at all what I would have expected from a middle-aged paleontologist. It didn't take long for me to discover, however, that Louise made a point of marching to her own drummer.

Intensity crackled around this woman like loose electrical cables. Obviously very bright, Louise had made a career out of focusing that intensity on work she pioneered nearly two decades earlier, while still in graduate school. All her life, Louise had loved fossils, loved the idea that they gifted modern scientists with a trail of clues to the distant past, clues that sometimes created a picture more detailed than the written history we rely on now. The thought that she could spend her life getting paid to research the topic she loved seemed to Louise like a dream come true.

Of course, that meant getting a Ph.D., a somewhat unlikely choice for a woman at the time. But then, paleontology was a somewhat unlikely choice to begin with. And by focusing all her intensity on her lifelong dream, Louise did it. The fossil research she began in graduate school looked like a promising way for oil companies to locate deposits. And much to her delight, a large oil company hired her to develop her ideas into reality.

Louise found herself in her element, free to focus her considerable talents and energy on the one topic she loved the most. And for
15 years, she did just that, specializing more and more, a sleuth hom-
ing in ever closer on the few tiny fossils that offered her clues. Louise
spent so much time with her nose in the dirt that she didn't pay much
attention when the company began developing other kinds of research projects, leasing additional lab space for experiments that used
electronic gadgets equipped with sound waves and sensitive meters.
She snorted when the company's new re-engineering expert, a wiry
young man who wore fragile round glasses, began raising questions
about the size of the oil deposits Louise had found. And she didn't
know that two competing oil companies had recently abandoned research projects much like hers in favor of other, newer techniques.

And so it came as a complete surprise when the vice president of
research called Louise to his office and told her they'd been forced to
abandon her project in favor of more productive, higher technology
methods—methods that Louise knew little about. He told her sadly
that he wished the company had another spot for her, a highly educated, obviously dedicated professional worthy of the company's respect and admiration. But she was so specialized in her area of
research that she just wouldn't fit in any other program. Louise and
her senior researchers had four weeks to finish up their projects and
clear out their lab space for the new team.

It took Louise a few days to rouse herself from the shock and dis-
belief—not to mention the insult. Hadn't she done exactly what the
company asked of her? Hadn't she found them oil deposits at a half-
dozen unlikely and previously unknown sites? Hadn't they implied,
through their years of faith in her work, that they would support her
efforts through retirement? She'd given the company the best 15
years of her professional life, and now they were done with her?

Worst of all, she soon discovered that all the other refiners had the
same reaction. Louise began her reluctant job search by writing to
three companies she considered prestigious enough to work for.
They politely declined. Nervous and defensive, she then sent out 10

résumés, to smaller companies. Not interested. And those that responded all said pretty much the same thing: Louise was too specialized in an area of expertise that had gone out of date. She'd need so much retraining that it was more worth their while to hire younger scientists, less experienced than she but more familiar with the high-tech world of the future.

Months later, defeated and more indignant than ever, Louise took a $35,000 pay cut to teach paleontology part-time at a local junior college. Aside from the shocking loss of income, she felt a deep and painful loss of dignity. Plus, she found that she didn't enjoy teaching young people. As a group, they seemed uninterested and unwilling to learn. Many of them handed assignments in late, simply assuming that she'd take them when she got them. In her anger, Louise began making enemies, insulting the administrators and alienating her students instead of attracting them to the topic. People began to think of Louise as a difficult, argumentative person, and they began to tell her so. Worried that even her new lower-paying job was now on the line, a despondent Louise called my office.

The Fate of a Specialist

Louise made a number of career choices understandable in an earlier time but unwise in this era. In the academic world of Louise's past, the phrase "publish or perish" ruled a career. These days, in business, the unspoken credo of a growing number of companies is, "progress or perish." But instead of positioning herself on the cutting edge of new technology, Louise—at 45 years old—had allowed herself to get stuck in a blind alley, a professional box canyon that employers didn't think she had the time or energy to climb out of. She lost her skills as a generalist; consequently, she lost her ability to command a job in her rapidly changing field. Her employer encouraged her to develop very specific, esoteric skills, then left her feeling betrayed when those skills fell by the industry's wayside.

This feeling of betrayal springs from another career choice understandable at the time but unwise now. The crux of the matter is that Louise made an assumption. She reached the conclusion in her own mind that her employer would support her work throughout her professional life. In essence, she saw her employer as the provider of a perpetual grant. She didn't see the corporate trend toward cost containment and resource justification, not because the signs weren't there, but because she didn't want to.

The surprise Louise felt at her termination was rooted in yet another problem whose solution would have been well within her control. She wasn't networked well enough into her company or her industry to see the writing on the wall. Louise focused fiercely on her job and, by anyone's standards, did it very well. But she neglected to develop professional relationships that might have influenced her future. These are expectations and decisions that Louise could have controlled—decisions that, in this day and age, we *must* control.

Taking Charge

How can you know which aspects of your career are within your control and which are outside your control? How can you prepare yourself for a future that isn't here yet? Of course, there are no complete or perfect answers to these questions. But I believe that, if you start with a few basic principles, you'll get plenty of directional signals along the way. And you'll feel as though you've taken control of your life—the parts of your life that you can and should control—at a time when most of us feel less in control than ever.

The first step in taking charge of your working life is in understanding and accepting that your career is up to you. It's your burden to bear, your race to run. No one else can do it. No one else *will* do it. For a long time, we've been able to think of our employers as parental figures committed to taking care of us, providing for us well beyond our working lives. To survive in today's business world, we must let go of that thought. This has become the time of the expendable worker—the time when you may get kicked out of the nest before you're ready to go. If you're not prepared, the landing can be very hard, even if you're one of the lucky few suspended by a golden parachute.

Many experts these days are beginning to say that you have to start thinking of yourself as self-employed, an entrepreneur (no matter whom you work for), or a free agent. The point they're all making is that the only one who can take care of you is you. The only one who can decide which direction is right for you is you. If you're not paying attention, if you're not supervising and watching out for your own career, who will? If you're not making choices about your own future, who can you blame if you end up in a job you don't want? Or if you end up with no job at all? We each carry the responsibility for our own lives.

For many people, the really difficult part of this era of downsizing is the sense of powerlessness, the feeling that you can work a long time for a company and simply get fired. But if you think of yourself as a free agent, as your own employer, then you can gain a new sense of influence over your career. You are not simply at the mercy of an outside force. You are progressing along a path of your own choosing, and the company you work for is leasing your skills and knowledge from you because those qualities have value. If that company takes a different path, you may lose your lease. But if you've chosen your field wisely and kept your skills well honed, you'll be just as valuable to plenty of other employers. And if you've put some money aside, planning for periods of unemployment, you can even keep the financial anxieties at bay.

The second step in taking charge is to embrace the fact that a lifetime of working for a single employer is, for most people, a thing of the past, a myth. We can no longer make assumptions about our employers. We can no longer expect promises—implicit or outright—that an employer will take care of its workers, financially, physically, emotionally, up to and through retirement. If it happens, great. But we can't expect that.

Of course, if you work a long time for a company and you lose

Thinking Like a Free Agent

A growing number of consultants these days are telling us to think of ourselves as being self-employed, to feel that we're working for ourselves no matter who signs the paycheck. John Challenger, executive vice president of the well-known Chicago-based outplacement firm Challenger, Gray & Christmas, says that's a step in the right direction. But it may not go far enough. Instead, he says we should think of ourselves as free agents.

"In fact," he says, "if you're working for a company, you're *not* self-employed. You are not autonomous. You need to commit to that organization and to the people around you while you work there. But if you think of yourself as self-employed, that loyalty and commitment may be hard to create."

If you're a free agent, Challenger says, you can think of yourself as retaining the right to move to a new opportunity, to stay open to new opportunities, indeed to invite new opportunities. But you can still base your career on quality work, loyalty to the company, commitment to the company's vision—values excellent employees have always espoused.

In most cases, this approach creates a win-win situation. The company gets a loyal, hard-working employee, and you get to take charge of your career. "You could be doing a wonderful job and, because of some corporate phenomenon, still find that you're out of a job," explains Challenger. "If you think of yourself as a free agent, you can base your working life on some of those good values that employees used to have, while still taking care of yourself."

your job, you have every right and reason to spend time grieving, being angry, and getting over the shock. It *is* a shock. But eventually you have to come to a decision. Either you can take charge of your career, bring your skills up to date, and take your own initiative, or you can spend your life angry and frustrated that your employer did you wrong. I don't know about you, but that doesn't sound like much of a life to me. Don't misunderstand. This can be a very hard time in a person's life. And everyone requires a different amount of time to heal. But in the final analysis, if you sit quietly and look closely, you'll see that destroying the rest of your life over an action taken by your employer is your choice. It's not your employer's fault. You are the only one who can destroy the rest of your life. Or you can try to make it even better than it was before.

Lifelong Learning

The third, and arguably the most important, principle for taking charge of your career is accepting the challenge of lifelong learning. Once you embrace the thought that you are the only one responsible for your career, and that you probably will not work all your life for one employer, the natural next question is this: What can I do to make sure I have a future? The answer is lifelong learning.

It's quite clear in today's marketplace that you are no longer guaranteed permanent employment. But even though a company won't guarantee you future employment, it can and should guarantee you the freedom to ensure your own future employability. After all, this process is in everyone's best interest, including the company you work for.

Future employability is based on your ability and motivation to learn. It's based on your up-to-the-minute knowledge and state-of-the-art skills and experience. Obtaining these qualities is well within your control—and forms the foundation of your attractiveness to employers. You are the master of your professional standards. You set the bar. But your employer will judge the height. That's why your employer must cooperate in your quest to learn and grow in your field.

Usually, of course, this is no problem. In fact, the more you learn, the more you bring to your employer. This works out well for both of you. But in the rare instance when you find that you're not learning new things at work, and you have no avenue to learn new things, I'd suggest that you start looking for other employment options because, over the long haul, you will become obsolete to the very employer who's now holding you back. And you'll be even farther behind your colleagues at other companies who did stay up to date.

It's completely up to you to guard this process of learning and acquiring skills that you can take with you from job to job. You're responsible for your life. You're responsible for your retirement. You're responsible to get as much as you can out of every single job you hold. If your company is not providing that opportunity for you, make it clear that that's what you need. If your company still won't provide it for you, choose a bright future over a dead-end present. Start looking for the time and the method to say goodbye.

Also keep in mind that, although any learning is a step in the right direction, you should try to learn as many *transferable* skills as possible. Louise learned a great deal over the years about the fossils she was studying, but the rest of the refining world was concentrating on different skills, leaving her literally in the dust. To stay current, you have to pick your head up, look around, see what the rest of your industry is doing. Listen to what your employer's executives are talking about. Learn how to do jobs besides your own. The very worst thing you can do is simply put your nose to the grindstone and refuse to think about it. It's up to you to accumulate portable knowledge and permanent connections at each job you hold. Even though the company can take your job away from you, it can't take what's in your head or in your network of colleagues.

Back to School

Sometimes in talking with middle-aged people I find that they feel tricked, discontented, and disgruntled about this topic of lifelong learning. After all, by the time we reach middle age, we're supposed to be established in our careers, getting ready to start resting on our laurels—certainly not going back to school, taking initiative, and continually redeciding what to do with life. But technology is changing so fast that, these days, you can't stop learning for even a minute, no matter how old you are or how established you are in your career. Once, it seemed that you could get through your whole career with what you learned in school and what you learned on the job. Not any more. Not if you want to ensure future employment. Today, even people at the top of their field must constantly update and expand their skills and knowledge to stay current.

A Greek philosopher once said that you can't step in the same river twice. In today's world of high technology, you can't step in the same river once, because while you're stepping down, the river is rushing past under your feet. Don't be lulled into thinking this trend won't hurt you if you don't currently have a high-tech job. Technology is altering everything about our way of life, in every field, every minute of the day, in virtually every job. If it hasn't touched you yet, it will. It won't be long until computer literacy is practically mandatory for getting a job, the lowest common denominator for employment. If you can't use a computer, put this book down, go find a community college schedule, and sign up for a class. If you can't afford a class, ask a friend for help. Or go to the library and sign up for computer assistance. While you're waiting, read a basic book about computers. There are no excuses any more for thinking of computers as alien creatures. In fact, they are integral to our lives and our futures.

So how do you get started on this quest for lifelong learning? Start with your attitudes. Start with willingness. Start by asking questions. Develop a curiosity about the work world bustling around you. Don't expect miracles at first. If you've spent all your time working at your own job and never learned a range of skills or interests, learning will seem difficult at first. It's analogous to muscles when you don't use them. They lose strength and quickness—temporarily. That's why everything seems so hard when you first start an exercise program. But the more you exercise, the easier it becomes. Likewise, the more you exercise your mind and your learning skills, the easier mental exercise will become for you. That's the way human bodies and minds work.

Also, you have to be willing to face reality, and to be alert to change. You have to be willing to retool as the future becomes the present, and to think of that retooling as a benefit, a conquest, and a necessary part of your future employability. Coincidentally, all this learning and retooling may well give a boost to your future happiness. Studies have repeatedly shown that people stay happier and healthier well into old age if they keep learning and growing.

Keep in mind, however, that different people learn in different ways. Maybe you learn best when you hear information spoken aloud. Maybe you learn best when you read. Maybe you learn best by doing. Try to make use of whatever learning mechanism you find most comfortable and most effective. Find out what's going on in your industry and prepare yourself for a future where you are in charge of your choices and your reactions. Don't just accept, without questioning, what someone else says. Consider a number of different sources. Hopefully, as a result, you will become a critical thinker. The world needs more critical thinkers. Employers need more critical thinkers. Don't be too quick to run with the herd. Think. Consider. Be willing to hold, as compatible, concepts that seem contradictory. Accept that, usually, the truth is complex. This learning process is not simply about finding the right answers. It's also about learning to ask the right questions.

More in Control

This is the process that Louise and I tackled, and it wasn't long before she started exercising her critical thinking skills. As a scientist accustomed to asking questions, she took to it quickly. Eventually, she even came to see herself as part of the reason for her own layoff. On the day we talked about hitting rapids in the uncharted river of life, Louise smiled gently to herself and said, "Hitting rapids will be easier from now on because, next time, I won't demand that the river change course for me."

Who knows—in the future we might be really glad the river doesn't change course just because we want it to. Once again I find myself saying that the change taking place in corporate America could be the best thing that's ever happened to us. After major changes in the past, life for most people eventually improved. We have no reason to assume that won't happen this time.

In the meantime, however, you must take charge of your career. Make yourself the best you can be in the context and environment where you are. In my opinion, lack of responsibility at work and in the community is one of the major factors contributing to the decline of society as we wish it to be. So start with yourself. Take responsibility. Control what's in your power to control, and give up trying to control the rest. You can control that you do a good day's work every day. But you can't control the size or the speed of the raises or promotions you get as a result. Give that up. You also can't control the future directions your employer may take, or the future decisions your employer may make. Give up your focus on that as well. Concentrate on learning, on growing, on being the most responsible, employable, curious person you know, a person who's excited and interested in mastering new skills and knowledge. If you do, it's my prediction that you'll be the last to lose a good job and the first to find a new one.

4

First Things First

WHAT IS A GOOD JOB, anyway? In America, the answer to that question has typically rested on personal interpretation, a matter of individual interests, choices, and talents. The problem is that, in this day and age, many of us assume we don't have the right or the freedom to ask the question any more. *Any* job is a good job, we tell ourselves. Any frustration or insult is worth bearing as long as there's a job in it. Just getting that paycheck is worth the day's effort, even if the day is longer and harder than ever. It's understandable that our current job insecurity would make us think this way. But if you really look at it, you'll see that this mode of thinking is a mistake that will hurt you in the long run *and* the short run.

We all see the news stories. They seem to be everywhere, these tales of people who lose a good job and have a hard time finding a comparable one. This is scary stuff. But even today—maybe especially today—settling for a job that breaks your spirit and bruises your self-esteem will only lead to negative results for you and everyone close to you. Keep in mind that there's still a vast variety of jobs out there, with more created almost daily. Some jobs you can work from home. Others offer flex time. We have an incredible number of choices. A job that's draining and unpleasant for you may be rewarding and motivating for someone else. It's still, at least in part, a matter of finding that good fit between your personal desires, the work you do, and the people you do it with.

In the long run, knuckling under to a job you find demeaning and uninspiring won't help you develop a satisfying career and a life you can look forward to with pleasure. In the short run, if you feel forced to knuckle under, you've probably already experienced the creeping resentment, the feeling of being trapped in your job, the anger and distrust directed at your employer, the lackluster work you can't seem to improve. You're stuck in a conflict between your desires and the demands of your job.

The only way out of this maze of discontent is by asking yourself this crucial question and a few others: What is a good job for me? What does my work mean to me? What priorities do I want in my career and my life? What do I think is important? What do I want to accomplish in my life? What qualities do I value? How does my career fit with my life's goals? Asking these questions of yourself is no less important today than it was 20 years ago; in fact, our rapidly changing workplace makes asking them more important than ever. In reality, these rapid changes give us more choices today than we've ever had, new categories of work to choose from, and more control over the direction of our futures, even though the illusion is one of less control. But it takes some initiative. It takes willingness not only to ask the questions, but to follow through on the answers. It takes courage.

Good employers don't want an army of drones sullenly carrying out orders without thought or investment. Good employers want employees who are alive, curious, thinking, learning, working hard because they want to, not just because they're afraid of losing whatever job they can find. To do this, to accomplish your work in a way that's good for you and good for your employer (which ultimately increases the chance of continued good for you), you have to make some choices and decisions about who you are and who you want to be, what you want for yourself, what you're willing to do, and what will damage your identity so much that you'll refuse to do it. I would never suggest that these are simple choices, that the answers are absolute, or that you can always know the answers ahead of time. But if you don't at least think about it, if you aren't willing to consider the priorities you want to have, and be willing to stand up for them in front of your employer and your loved ones, you may well find yourself on an uncomfortable career path, feeling compromised, becoming a person you don't want to be. Look, for instance, at what happened to Bill and Wendy Reilly.

A Model Father

I'd been seeing Wendy Reilly every two weeks for a couple of years. Preppy and conservative, Wendy had what people years ago used to call a pixie haircut. More often than not, she came to her appointments wearing white sneakers and short socks, a long denim skirt, and a round-collared, light-colored blouse—outfits that, on her tiny frame, made her look barely larger than the elementary school students for whom she was librarian. Add to that her tendency toward shyness and her small, almost whispery voice, and Wendy sometimes seemed little more than a child herself. Though she was a kind and honest person with a surprising dash of wit, from a stranger's viewpoint Wendy probably seemed a little afraid of the world. Indeed, in some ways she was, for a number of good reasons that stretched all the way back into her childhood. Those reasons left her burdened with nagging anxieties and little confidence in her own ability to make decisions. It wasn't long before I began to wonder if Wendy's husband, Bill, was an unwitting partner in allowing her struggle to continue.

From Wendy's perspective, Bill was the one reason that *didn't* bring her to see me. A steady, predictable man, Bill provided Wendy with the feeling that she had a firm foundation, a strong building to crouch under in case a tornado touched down nearby. Wendy relied on Bill's strength more than I knew she should, never venturing far outside the reach of his rescue. For his part, Bill carried a grave sense of responsibility for the cohesiveness of their family, and he did his best to provide financially and emotionally for their well-being. Most of their friends thought Bill seemed considerably older than his 36 years.

Wendy told me proudly that Bill was a model father. Every morning, he fixed breakfast for their twin boys so Wendy could get ready for school. After the boys boarded their bus and Wendy drove away, Bill finished getting ready for his own job as quality control manager for a small business that made parts for machines, motors mostly. This responsibility he shouldered stolidly as well, tending carefully to all the details and faithfully inspecting the company's wares. Every evening he left work right on time so he wouldn't risk ruining dinner with Wendy and the kids. After dinner and a little game time, he'd help the boys take baths and get into bed. He and Wendy took turns reading them their favorite bedtime stories.

For most of their nine married years, Bill called Wendy every day, just before leaving work, to tell her he was on his way home. "Love you," he always said reassuringly, just before hanging up. Wendy says the last time she heard him say those words is now etched more clearly in her memory than the day she gave birth. Because on that day, Bill said, "I have to get some cash, honey. I'll be home in about an hour. Love you." But in hindsight, Wendy told me that his inflection seemed different, more urgent somehow, as though he was straining to convince her.

He didn't come home in an hour. Or a day. Or a week. Or a month. Bill simply disappeared.

No Way Out

What Wendy didn't know—and I didn't know—until months later was that Bill's boss, the owner's eldest son, had been making veiled suggestions for Bill to fudge some figures on two of the machine parts he was responsible for inspecting. Not a lot. Just a little fudge to make things come out even. From what Wendy had told me, however, I knew two things very clearly about Bill. One was that he would resist fudging numbers, even a tiny bit, on principle. Bill was highly ethical, a deacon in his church, a man of integrity. He just wouldn't think it right. Second, Bill would never overlook mistakes that could hurt someone. And in his opinion, putting these parts into motors just might hurt someone. So, with worry and conflict rising high in his throat, Bill stalled. Frozen with fear, he didn't do anything. And he didn't tell anyone. In response, his boss quietly turned up the heat.

It started with Bill's performance review, which declined remarkably from previous reviews, and with Bill's raise, which didn't happen. Unsettled and uncertain, Bill didn't know what to do. But he felt that he couldn't—and shouldn't—tell Wendy. It would only upset her. And he couldn't find the words to tell the owner something so bad about his son.

But then Bill's boss told him to fire the five employees whose finished parts didn't pass inspection. Bill was appalled. Those people didn't work for him. And the quality of their parts stemmed directly from the quality of their manufacturing equipment, which the owner's son refused to upgrade.

For Bill, the pressure became enormous. His conscience wouldn't allow him to carry out his orders at work. And his feelings of responsibility for his family wouldn't allow him to openly defy his boss. After all, he might lose the job that kept him as the foundation of his family's stability. He felt as though walls were collapsing around him and he had no way out. Pulled between his principles and his allegiance to his family, Bill snapped.

Of course, when Bill disappeared, his family knew none of this. They knew only that their husband and father had vanished. Like any family would, they panicked. They called the police. They hired private detectives. A posse of professionals searched, to no avail. Months went by, and the family began to wonder if Bill were dead. Wendy grew depressed and distracted—so distracted, in fact, that she became an easy target for a mugger.

He was a polite-looking but dirty young man, and he knocked lightly on her car window while she sat at a red light. Not thinking, Wendy gently clicked the button that opened her window automatically, all the way. Just as she began to react to the man's left hand coming toward her, his right hand crashed forward too, bludgeoning her in the head with a rock. In little more than a moment, he yanked open her car door, pulled her to the pavement, grabbed her purse, and ran. Only later, sobbing in my office, did she wonder out loud what might have happened to the two little boys in the back seat with their hands over their mouths.

After nearly seven months of looking, savings depleted and emotionally exhausted, Wendy was wondering if she should give up when one of the private detectives called to say he'd located Bill. This responsible husband and family man—Wendy's rescuer—was in Honolulu, living with a local woman and working in a produce shop. At first, Wendy didn't believe it. That could not be my husband, she thought. Bill would never do that to us. It must be some cruel mistake.

But it was Bill. For several weeks he refused to even acknowledge Wendy's attempts to contact him. When she finally arrived unannounced at his door, Wendy found a man she didn't recognize—a man who, on the outside, didn't seem to care about anything or anyone. But in the moment when he looked her square in the eye, Bill let Wendy see the tortured man inside. And he began to tell her the story that, eventually, she brought back to me.

Would things have turned out differently if Bill had spoken honestly with Wendy and his employer? What will happen to Bill's children and their thoughts about life and relationships? Could this family's tragedy have been avoided? I believe that talking it out would have helped Wendy become the stronger person she was working toward. I also believe that Wendy could have shouldered some of the burden her husband tried to bear alone, possibly preventing his irreparable decision. But because of the way the story unfolded, no one will ever know the full answers to these questions, or the dozens of others swirling in Wendy's mind. I can say one thing with certainty, however. In much less dramatic, much more subtle ways, tragedies like this one happen every day. They happen when we try to compromise who we are and what's important to us, just to keep a job.

The Meaning of Work

At this time in our history, when jobs have become unstable and work is increasingly associated with anxiety, many of us are trying to simply press on—to put our heads down and do our jobs, hoping to survive the next tidal wave of reorganizing or downsizing. We're trying to meet our employers' increasing demands, trying to avoid the worst of the conflicts, bending our personal wishes and desires into submission while hanging onto the shrinking security a job can offer. We're simply working, trying to deflect the impact of that work from our lives and our thoughts about ourselves. We're telling ourselves, "It's just a job. I can survive this for 8 hours (or 10, or 12) and then I get to go home." Thus we're stuck between the need for a job and the desire to be happier at it.

At a time when jobs seem less secure than ever, this way of thinking is understandable. But the fact is that it won't get you where *you* want to go. It may get you where your employer wants you to go. But do you want to entrust your personal development—indeed, your future—to an employer? Even the best of employers, those who feel their success is ultimately linked with yours, couldn't possibly know you well enough to see what you want for your life, what matters most to you. Nor would they want that responsibility. You're the only one who can shoulder that responsibility. And you're the only one who can keep yourself from working at a job that drains and defeats you.

Of course, plenty of people these days are still happy in their work, motivated and energized by it. Not every working person in America is miserable, not by a long shot. But I would suggest to you that the people who are happiest in their work are the people whose jobs match most closely with who they are, what they want, and where they've set their priorities. If you're one of those people, congratulations. This is a lesson you may not have to learn right now. However, if you're not one of those people and you want to be, you can start by walking yourself through the process of defining the meaning and the role of work in your life—and by responding to what you find out about yourself.

Not Just a Job

The problem with thinking of a job as "just a job" is that it ignores the very real contribution that work makes to your life. One of Freud's beliefs, which I happen to agree with, is that love and work are the two most important aspects of a person's life. They each have a profound impact on your future and your feelings about yourself. They each have the potential to greatly increase—or greatly decrease—your sense of satisfaction with yourself and your life.

For this reason, it's important to recognize that your job is more than just a job. In fact, I would urge you to begin thinking of your job and your life's work as two distinct but related concepts. Think of your job as the vessel that holds your work. Think of your job as the venue in which that work takes place. Your work is part of who you are, translated into something you do; your job is the setting in which you do it.

Work is something, almost anything, that you have a desire to achieve. It's a constellation of tasks and effort that, considered as a whole, contains value for you as a person. Your life's work should be an accomplishment that, at its core, runs parallel to what you find important at your core. Your work can be raising a family, tending a garden, painting landscapes. It doesn't have to be a paying job in the traditional sense. Most of us, however, are trying to combine the financial security of a job with the feeling of accomplishment that comes through doing our life's work. In general, we want our work to happen at our jobs.

This definitely does not mean, however, that you are what you do. We Americans have a great tendency to fall into this mode of thinking, particularly in those careers where society offers great financial rewards. This is wrong-headed thinking, and it sets you up for personal disaster if your job should disappear. After all, if you think of yourself and your job as one, who are you without your job? I've helped many patients in their struggle to regain a sense of self after losing a job, and living by the phrase "I am what I do" only makes the process more agonizing.

Even if you're happy at your job, it's helpful to think of it as the place where you accomplish your work. It's useful to be clear about what that work is, about the important things your job is allowing you to accomplish. So when you say to someone, "I am a police officer," you know that what you really mean is, "I am a person who wants to protect those who need it, and I'm accomplishing that work through my job as a police officer." Or if you say to someone, "I am a school teacher," you know that what you really mean is, "I am a person who cares about helping our children fulfill their potential, and I'm accomplishing that work through my job as a school teacher."

Do you see the distinction? There's a difference between who you are and what you do. But you'll probably find the highest level of satisfaction with your job (what you do) if it's in line with at least some of the things you care deeply about (who you are). In short, your work should be something that, at some level, reflects your core values and talents. It should be important to you beyond simply paying the bills.

A Good Match

Why should we spend time splitting hairs over the difference between your job and your work? Because it helps you focus on you rather than on your job. It helps you begin thinking about what's important for you, about what has meaning for you, independent of your employer's goals and expectations. If you find that your deepest feelings and priorities run counter to what you're charged with doing every day at your job, that's a good reason to start thinking about a *career* change. If you find that your job matches pretty well with your sense of what's important, but your employer's policies and business goals hamper your ability to accomplish it, that's a good reason to start thinking about a *job* change. And if you confirm that your job allows you to spend time every day doing something you think is important and useful, something that has personal meaning for you, that's a good reason to start thinking about a *mental* change toward the positive.

Discovering that you and your job are in alignment opens the door to your own motivation. You aren't going off to work every day simply because your employer demands it; you're also going to fulfill your own needs and desires. If you feel that there's a certain work you want to accomplish, you can be more mentally invested in the job that allows you to accomplish it. You feel less drag. You can be more motivated, more committed, more willing to take responsibility and initiative at your job, because it's consonant with the work you know you want to do. This is good for you and for your employer. It's a good match. If you don't have that good match, start looking for ways to find it. You don't have to do anything rash or uncomfortable. But you do need to start establishing priorities in your own mind, priorities that you can begin to implement as opportunities arise.

Thinking of your job and your work as two distinct concepts yields another big bonus if your job should happen to go away— because even if it does, you still have your work. You still have purpose, even if you don't have that particular job in which to carry it out. Thinking this way won't erase the emotional aftermath of losing a job, but it does help. It helps you focus your search for another job. It helps you express your motivation and commitment to prospective employers. It helps you explain the connection between your last job and your next one. And it helps you understand and believe that, even if your job went away, you and the things that

are important to you did not. You can find those important things
again, in another job or another way of life.

What's Important?

How do you decide what's really important to you about your work
and, consequently, about your job? That's still a largely personal interpretation, based on the individual interests, choices, and talents
that develop and change throughout your life. But from a mental
health perspective, there are some principles you can use as guides in
reaching your conclusions.

Probably the most important one is that you can't underestimate
the impact of your work, and your job, on your life. Work is intimately tied to your concept of self and your satisfaction with life. It's
a major source of self-esteem. Your job provides you with personal
autonomy and a social connection outside your family. It helps you
establish a daily reality and routine. It fulfills the normal, human need
to be needed, to have a purpose. It gives you a forum in which to express your creativity and individuality. Your ability to hold a job, earn
a living, and work cooperatively with other people goes hand in hand
with good mental health. No wonder the loss of a job can be a major
blow. A job is indeed more than just a job.

However, the second most important principle is that your work
is not the whole of your life. This is another one of those seemingly
contradictory truths. Work is important enough to devote yourself
to; but a job is not important enough to devote your life to. There's
so much more to life than that. There's family, learning, hobbies,
mentoring, friendship, helping, teaching. If your work becomes all-
consuming, these valuable aspects of life can get squeezed out. Don't
trade your life for a job.

Another important principle is that work is not just about making
money. There's no doubt that a certain amount of money is necessary
to provide you with food, shelter, and other necessities of life. But
once you get beyond that, you can start reexamining your priorities.

To put it another way, there's a minimum level of income that you may have to spend all your energy trying to attain. But once you've attained it, the benefits of trying to continually increase it drop off. We've all heard the stories of unhappy lottery winners and miserable rich people. While it's silly to think that money makes you unhappy, once you obtain enough to provide for yourself and your family, more does not necessarily make you happier. And living only to get more may rob you of the other riches life can offer.

The last principle in deciding what's important to you about work is to be willing to really look, to have the courage to consider what's important to you even if it means deciding you're in the wrong job, and to be willing to consider what you really want to do, independent of how much it pays. For most people, even those who claim to love work, a job can be a great distraction to keep from thinking about what's really important. It's easy to let habit and inertia take over, to exist on autopilot without taking time to evaluate what you really think about your job and the course of your future. That may be in part because many of us simply assume that the more money you earn, the better your job. Or it could be because many of us assume that work is supposed to be drudgery. But if you can find that good match between who you are and what you do, work doesn't have to be drudgery at all. And the size of the paycheck may become secondary to the joy of the job.

Setting Boundaries

Once you begin to decide what's important to you about your work, you can also begin to set boundaries around the tasks involved in that work. By knowing what matters to you, you'll be better able to determine whether a new direction at work is the right or wrong direction for you. You'll be able to base your decisions on a world view, a life view, that you've actually thought about. You'll have some idea of what—to you—is worth dying (or not dying) for, divorcing (or not divorcing) for, quitting (or not quitting) for, standing up (or not standing up) for. The boundaries you set for yourself in all areas of life form the framework for who you are. They are worth very careful consideration.

Why do we need to set boundaries at work? Because in the work setting these days, competition and the drive for success has made employers ask more from us than ever before. Plus, the technology explosion now presents us with a potentially endless work day connected to pagers, mobile phones, laptops, car faxes, and home offices. If you let it, your work could monopolize you seven days a week, 24 hours a day. It's up to you to decide how to respond to these pressures, based on your priorities and what's important in your life. Many times, you may choose to do exactly what your employer asks, even if it means relocating or working more hours. But if you simply assume that you must do everything your employer asks, you may find yourself trading your life for your job. At some point, wherever you set your boundary, you may need to find a way to say no.

Every person sets boundaries at different places. One of my patients reached the end of her rope when her employer shifted her job to an outlying plant, which would have meant an extra two hours of commuting each day. She felt this would place too big a strain on her children, already in day care almost 10 hours a day, so she began looking for another job and eventually quit. A patient who worked for a computer company felt driven to quit because, in her estimation, her employer gave her tools inadequate to do her job well. Yet another had enough when he was introduced to his eleventh boss in the space of a year. An HMO physician I know felt worse and worse about his job as the demand to see more and more patients grew. So he joined a different group of doctors and, though he's making less money now, he's treating each patient with the care and concern he thinks important. Finally, there's the cashier who loved her job mainly because of the conversations she had with people throughout the day. Then her employer installed a computer-monitored register and required her to increase her speed so much she hardly had time to say hello. She applied for a customer service job when it came open, and now happily spends her days personally solving customer problems. These people all figured out how to respond to what they knew were priorities in their lives. They're good examples of the notion that sound mental health is built on flexibility and adaptability to your changing environment and personal needs.

I've also had patients unwilling to stand by their priorities. One patient, who worked some 80 hours a week and now says he gave his life to his company, labored through two heart attacks, two divorces, and the loss of many neglected friends. When he was laid off, he wrongly blamed the squandering of his life on his employer. Another patient dissolved into tears while describing the year of her biggest promotion as the year she abandoned her children. Certainly, this woman did not literally abandon her children. She provided for them in many wonderful ways. But she felt that she'd been overly devoted to her work and later blamed herself for the problems her children developed as teenagers. She was angry and she was guilt-ridden. She wondered why she hadn't considered her career decisions more carefully.

The short message here is that you are not trapped. You have some control over what you will and won't do. If you're motivated and committed to the work you've established for yourself, you don't have to settle for any old job just to have one. You can take your skills and your motivation to another employer who'll be happy to have you. Or you can become your own employer if you want to. Usually, the person hardest to convince about all this is you. Many of us stay in jobs we don't like out of habit, a desire for security, the length of time we've invested, inertia, fear of the unknown, the sense of not deserving better—for lots of reasons, some of them good, some not so good. I'm certainly not suggesting that you quit your job because there's something you don't like about it. There will *always* be something you don't like about your job. What I'm suggesting runs much deeper than that. I'm suggesting that you will end up unhappy if you ignore who you are and the things you think are important, simply to keep a job.

More often than not, you probably won't need to exercise your willingness to leave. Usually, the knowledge that you could and would leave your job if you had to simply adds to your personal sense of freedom. It gives you the guts to speak up, to ask to modify your job with your current employer. I believe that, in most cases, if you can demonstrate to an employer the mutual benefits of allowing you to do what motivates you most, you'll get the green light to do it. It's up to you to bring your job in line with what you think is important—and to bring added value to your employer at the same time.

Reevaluate Your Future

It's always uncomfortable to think about taking a risk, making a wave, changing jobs, even if your job is bad for you. What you may not realize, however, is that you take an enormous risk by keeping the status quo. Consider the woman who stays with an abusive partner because she risks loneliness by leaving. What she hasn't considered is the risk that staying with the abuser could prevent her from meeting a wonderful new partner. Or the risk that staying with her abuser could prevent her from her discovering her own strength and resilience in an independent life. Keep in mind that there are risks on both sides of a decision. There are risks to changing your job, and there are risks to continuing in a job that squashes who you are.

So, far from being less able to ask the questions, these days we must ask ourselves more than ever: What do I want? Where do I want to end up? Is my job taking me closer to or farther away from what I think is important? If you don't ask questions like these, our rapid corporate current will take you where it wants to take you, whether you really want to go there or not.

Many of us have strong feelings about work but relatively few clear ideas about it. And some of our behaviors prevent us from gaining those clear ideas. For one thing, many of us aren't sleeping enough to be fully awake. Instead of sleeping to satisfy our own internal clocks, we set alarms to meet the demands of the work world.

To make matters worse, more of us than ever are traveling across multiple time zones, upsetting our circadian rhythms, then expecting to perform at full mental power the next morning. This is not reasonable.

Another problem is our culture's obsession with time. These days, doing something every waking minute is no longer enough. We want to do two, three, four things at once to make the best use of time. We want to be constantly busy, working, moving, getting somewhere, anywhere, "ahead" by the shortest route possible. Did you ever ask yourself what getting "ahead" means to you?

When it comes to asking yourself questions like the ones we've discussed here, I would suggest that you stop. Reflect. Observe your life and define your work and consider your job. Stop going for a minute so you can see where you're going. Your work can make a legitimate and deep contribution to your life. Does it? Your work can help you feel fulfilled and purposeful. Does it? Your work can make you feel motivated and give you the initiative you need to take hold of each day. Does it?

If you're willing to do some soul-searching, and you're willing to stand up for what you believe, and you're willing to give your best effort to the job that supports your work, you'll gain satisfaction for the most important person of all—yourself.

5

Saved by a Net

CREATING SOME LEVEL of synergy between who you are and what you do is central to feeling good about your work. It's the prerequisite for building a sense of satisfaction in that very important area of your life. As you've seen, you're the only one who can define that synergy for yourself. After all, it's based almost entirely on your personality, your interests, your desires, your preferences. All these characteristics are unique to you. However, even though the process of attaining *satisfaction* rests squarely on your shoulders, the process of attaining *success* does not. Success in one's career is rarely a solitary accomplishment, especially in this time of rapid change and expanding globalization. More and more these days, attaining success in your field results from hard work, a commitment to lifelong learning, *and* connections with other people. To achieve *satisfaction*, you need a connection between who you are and what you do. In general, to achieve *success* and keep it, you need a multitude of meaningful connections between you and others.

I'm talking about networking. I'm talking about cultivating relationships for the purpose of mutual benefit. I'm talking about what business leaders these days call strategic alliances. Even major companies, highly competitive in their fields, are now scrambling to form such alliances with other companies, here and abroad—alliances designed to benefit all partners and open new doors to growth, new paths into the future, and new sources of competitive strength. As individuals, we need to take a lesson from the people who run these companies, from the people who understand that we all make more progress when more of us are pulling in the same direction.

For many of us, this mind-set is a foreign concept. We've grown up in a society that fosters individual competition—at school, on the playing field, in the workplace. Someone wins and someone else loses. Someone moves ahead and someone else falls back. In general, we each want to be the one who wins, and we want to win on our own. We have not grown up revering collaboration and teamwork. In this time of massive downsizing, sometimes we even begin to think of our coworkers as competitors rather than compatriots. Someone keeps a job, and someone else loses one. From a mental health perspective and, increasingly, from a business perspective, this way of thinking isn't helpful. In fact, mental health experts now know that the more meaningful connections you have with other people, the healthier you're apt to be. And business experts are finding that, the more connections you have with other people in your field and related ones, the more *successful* you're apt to be. Consider the example of Jan and Larry.

A Tale of Two Patients

Jan and Larry both worked for the same large health-care company, in different departments and in different buildings. To my knowledge, they didn't know each other. But they were both my patients. I'd been seeing Larry for a couple of months and Jan for more than a year when I read in the newspaper that their employer had been taken over by a larger company headquartered in a different state. I wondered how the takeover would affect these two hardworking people, especially Jan.

Something of a loner, Jan spent her days on a telephone headset, answering questions for members of the company's health plan. She had little time to socialize at work because as soon as one call ended, another came through. She could barely make time to take her full half-hour lunch break. Jan was a single mother and thought she should spend as much time as possible with her shy 3-year-old. So she arrived at work right on time, and she didn't hang out to chat after hours. In fact, Jan told me she hardly knew the people she worked with. She simply came to work, gave a good day's effort, and went home.

Larry, on the other hand, was an affable young man who carefully watched and participated in the events unfolding around him. Engaged to a woman who was still away at college, Larry had few competing responsibilities. So he went out for a beer a few times a week with one or more of his colleagues. He played on the company softball team. And he founded a company-wide recycling program. Larry had his share of problems, but being able to talk with and relate to other people wasn't one of them. I got the impression that he knew most of the company's managers, a fair share of the executives, and, through his evening outings and the softball team, he even got to know some competitors.

In fact, in Jan and Larry's city, five large health-care companies competed against each other. It wasn't at all unusual for an employee to leave one company and go to work for a competing one. So when Larry went to the local watering hole or to a softball game with his colleagues, often as not he ended up talking about work, sometimes with former employees—continued friends—who had gone to work for competitors.

Not long after the takeover, rumors began to circulate that the parent company intended to come in and "reduce redundancy." Since they already performed many of the same functions at the national headquarters, it seemed they didn't need a number of the departments Jan and Larry's company had. The downsizing was drastic. Jan and Larry lost their jobs on the very same day, with no warning and no recourse. Because neither had worked for the company very long, they received little in the way of severance pay.

Jan took the opportunity to keep her son home from day care while she scanned the paper for other jobs and tinkered with her resume on the computer. Every day, she sent out a few resumes and waited for a phone call. Though she had confidence that she'd find another job, Jan told me that the isolation in her apartment sometimes felt overwhelming. She adored her son, of course, but a 3-year-old can provide only a limited amount of real companionship for an adult. She couldn't leave him alone in the apartment while she looked for a job, and she didn't have anyone to watch him for an hour here and there while she went for interviews. Eventually, she decided to put him back in day care for the morning or the afternoon if she had an interview. But the added expense only worsened her fear of running out of money.

Larry, on the other hand, showed up at a softball game the day after his layoff, much to the chagrin of the personnel director. But Larry didn't blame or badmouth his former employer. He simply watched the game, leaning forward in the bleachers, cheering and clapping with the rest of the crowd. When the game ended and he went out to congratulate the crowd of players, Larry pulled one young manager of a competing company off to the side and said, "Now that I'm a free agent, I want to give you an idea I proposed at my old job. My boss didn't go for it, but if you want to try it, great. I think it might save you guys some money." After listening to the idea, the young man clapped Larry on the back and said, "Hey, thanks a lot. That might work."

Four days later, when Larry got home from his morning run, he found a message on his answering machine. It was the personnel director of that young manager's company, and he asked Larry to please return his call. It turned out that the manager had a job coming open on his staff, a job no one even knew about yet, and he wondered if

Larry wanted to come in for an interview. A week later, Larry had a job offer. A week after that, he was back at work, playing softball for someone else's team. Larry found out a month or two later that his idea didn't work. But by then he'd had enough other ideas to make up for it.

Jan eventually got a job too, as a receptionist at a local attorney's office. But she had a longer row to hoe before she got it. Without any contacts or assistance, it took her nearly four months to find a new job. In the meantime, she had to live on cash advances from her credit cards. She told me it would probably take about a year to pay off the debt. But she said she was glad to have a job she thought she'd enjoy, and she was happy that the pay was similar to her old job. She just wished it hadn't taken so long to find.

Meaningful Connections

In my observation, the people best able to weather adversity are those with a multitude of meaningful connections. Jan and Larry illustrate this concept very well. Larry once told me that he wanted to build a strong network of family, friends, and acquaintances so that, if he ever started falling, he'd have a net to save him. Indeed, it did. It saved him the emotional and financial stress of spending an extended period of time looking for a job. If Jan had built such a network, it might have lifted her mood, brightened her thoughts about the future, and provided joyous relief from her isolation—besides helping her find a new job.

The way the workplace is developing and changing these days, we need to forget about the ladder concept. The ladder, as we used to know it, has fallen. What we need now is a net, a web of connectedness. We need to think laterally, of teams and teamwork, instead of striving to move singularly up the hierarchy. The more people you know and can tap for knowledge and connections, the more likely you are to weather the next storm that comes along—and the more valuable you are as an employable person. Your value lies not only in your up-to-date knowledge and skills. It also lies in your social capital, your network of other knowledgeable people who can keep you informed and competitive.

Connections aren't just about getting another job. They're about learning and growing personally and professionally. They're about exchanging thoughts and knowledge with other thoughtful people. They're about friendship and moral support. They're about offering something of value, and feeling valuable yourself. For Jan, maybe they could have been about help with child care, or maybe even a low-interest loan.

Likewise, connections are not just for business colleagues. We need connections with immediate family members and extended family members. People of faith need connections at their place of worship. We all need connections with people who share our interests, our hobbies, our sorrows, our talents, and our personal histories. These connections enrich us, they spur us on, they comfort us, and— if we're falling—they just might catch us before we've fallen too far.

Things don't always work out perfectly even if you do have a broad network of colleagues, friends, and acquaintances. But they usually work out better. And they usually work out quicker.

Building a Network

Many of the people I talk with resist the concept of networking. It seems distasteful somehow, like hobnobbing or glad-handing. It smacks of fakery. But that's not what networking is at all. Networking should be an outgrowth of your genuine interests, not a snow job or a ploy to get people to help you. Networking is about pooling resources and pulling together for mutual benefit; remember, it's not about competition any more. It's about collaboration. It's about adding value to someone else's life, not just hoping for value in yours.

But how do you start networking if the concept is foreign to you? How do you overcome uneasiness and shyness to start enlarging your network of meaningful connections? How do you get over the discomfort at needing and wanting to learn something new? With Jan, we started slowly. Maybe you'll want to do the same thing.

Start by thinking about what you've accomplished in your life. Think about your achievements. Maybe you've worked quietly at the same job for 17 years. But on that job you must have learned some new things. And in your life outside of work, you also must have learned some new things. If you're like most people, you can probably isolate a number of important areas of growth and learning. You *can* grow. You *can* learn. So you really don't have to suffer an inordinate amount of fear about learning what you need to know now. You can do it. Right?

Now the issue is *how* to do it. Many people feel uncomfortable or anxious about striking up conversations with others they hardly know. So start small. The first week, make a point of smiling at everyone you pass in the hallway. The second week, keep smiling, and make a point of saying something to one person you don't know each day. Say something simple, like, "Hi. How are you?" When you say it, look at the person. Make sure the person knows you asked the question because you're interested. Expect an answer. Say something back. Pretty soon you're in a conversation. The third week try to have a small conversation with a couple of people you don't know. The point is to make yourself a series of graduated goals and check them off as you do them. If all goes well, your feelings of competence in this area will keep increasing as people respond positively to you.

Keep in mind that the chances they'll respond positively to you are quite high. Most people really want to be liked and appreciated. If in some way you can express your appreciation for another person without being saccharine or false, you will never be at a loss for acquaintances. The best thing to do is smile and be genuinely interested. After all, most people are interesting. Not long ago, one of my patients looked around at all the books in my office and said, "I don't read a lot, so I consider people to be my books. I learn something from every person I get to know." What a wonderful attitude.

Most people consider it a pleasant experience to have someone express an interest in who they are and what they do. Don't be nosy or obnoxious. Be sensitive to another person's moods and pressures. But be interested. Focus on the person. Don't worry about what that person thinks of you. Make yourself too busy thinking about that other person. Pretty soon, you may find that you're building a network.

Counting Friends

I can feel some of you balking, just like some of my patients do at this point. Make friends with the people at work? That sounds dumb, even dangerous. What if I lose my job? Will I lose my friends too? What if the people I consider my friends decide to blame me for something that goes wrong at work? What if they weren't really my friends after all? I didn't pick these people. I just work with them.

If you're thinking this way, you're still in the old competition mind-set. And you're making a false assumption that the people at work are somehow different from the people you'd choose as friends outside of work. They're not. And besides, how many other options do you have for developing friendships? Where else are you meeting and interacting with people? You probably spend the majority of your waking hours on the job. These people can and should become your friends.

Think about it this way. When you were a kid, where did you make friends? In your neighborhood, probably, and on the school yard. But you didn't pick the people who lived on your block or went to your school. You just found certain ones in the group you thought were interesting, people who appealed to you, and you made friends. It's the same thing at work.

The fact is that work is a social environment, one of the few remaining for many of us. From a mental health viewpoint, one of the biggest problems in America right now is a lack of community. An increasing number of us are living in gated neighborhoods. We lock our doors behind us. We have house alarms with signs to that effect posted in the front yard. Many of us don't know our neighbors. We bring pizza and a video home instead of going out with friends. How are you going to meet people? Work presents the most obvious choice for most of us. So once again, we come up against the idea that a job is not just a job. It's a whole network of relationships. It's support. It's perspective.

By the way, many corporate leaders grow nervous about employees who have a tight band of friends in the organization. Maybe this is partly paranoia on their part. Maybe it isn't warranted. But the best way to deal with it is to avoid giving them reasons to be nervous. Be respectful of the mutual trust you can build with your employer. Work hard. Take initiative. Don't chat with your friends about non-work issues during work time. You're getting paid to work. And don't use the size of your salary as an excuse either. I once had a patient say to me, "Well, they only pay me half a salary, so I only work half the time." The comment was funny, and we can probably all recognize the logic working here. But there are two problems with this way of thinking. First is that, presumably, you accepted the wage at the time you accepted the job. Second is that acting this way will never get you to a higher paying position, because you won't have demonstrated your ability and willingness to work. So keep in mind that, even as you build a network of colleagues, friends, and acquaintances, your responsibility at work is to work.

It's also useful to remember that, in this time of exploding business start-ups, you never know which of your colleagues will go out and start a thriving business. Do you want that person to remember you as a slacker who bellyached about work all day? Or do you want that person to remember you as someone who's a real asset to a business?

What this means in practical terms is that your interactions with colleagues will probably need to extend outside the bounds of the work day. If the person is worth it, go out of your way to invest in the friendship. Don't be a pest. But call. Get together for lunch. If you're going out with some colleagues, see if this person wants to go along. Even if the answer is no, the person will feel that you cared enough to ask. That feels good. That makes you feel like friends.

Even if you or some of your work friends get laid off, try to maintain those relationships. Make dates. Try to keep and enlarge the network you have rather than dropping existing friends as new ones come along. Of course, you'll start building a new set of friends if you move to a new job, but don't forget the old network. Pick a few people at your old job and stay in touch.

The larger the network of social connectedness you have, the longer you're likely to live. This has been studied by health experts. The people you have in your life exert a considerable influence on your physical and mental health. Be careful about those you consider your friends, of course. You don't want people around you who exert a negative influence. But this applies to people outside of work as well. Some people you can't trust as friends, most you can. So try to be reasonably optimistic and reasonably trusting. If it's meant to be that you're going to lose your job, you're going to lose it. You might as well leave a bunch of friends rather than a bunch of people you don't know.

One footnote: I can attest to the fact that depression is contagious. So is an upbeat, optimistic attitude. When you're choosing which people to hang out with, remember that smiling, happy people change your brain chemistry and your mood for the better. Likewise, negative, melancholy people can drag your thoughts and your mood toward their way of being. This doesn't mean you should shun sad or depressed people. It simply means that you should think about the people you spend the majority of your time with. Are these the people you want to resemble? The more time you spend with them, the more you'll be like them.

A Global View

To build a truly useful, fully functioning network of friends and acquaintances, you'll need to look beyond your circle at work. You'll need to cultivate relationships in other areas of your field and other areas of the map. Look for people outside your employer but inside your industry. Take a night class on a topic related to your work, and stay in touch with the teacher and any students who seem like good contacts. See if your company will send you to a conference or seminar related to your work, then make it your business to meet people there. And don't forget that, more and more, companies are taking a global view of competition and progress. It used to be that America was so far in the lead, we had to worry about competing only with ourselves. No more. We're still in the lead, but we're not so far ahead that we can afford to ignore competition from oncoming countries. Any international connections you can make will expand your thinking, help you build a more accurate world view, and possibly bode well for your continued employment. With the Internet available in everyone's home, making these global connections is easier than it's ever been. If you have an opportunity to learn a new language— Japanese, Spanish, Chinese—do it. You'll add even more value to your international connections.

The take-home message here is that insularity—in your house, in your job, in your mind—could ultimately reduce your chances of moving forward in this economic era. These days, patriotism has more than ever to do with cooperation. You have to acquire information and learn skills from every source, even if that source is half a world away. After all, successful companies buy from the place where they can get the best bid, no matter where in the world it is. As a result, there's a certain homogeneity developing among big cities all over the world. In fact, residents of big cities worldwide may have more in common with each other than they do with other citizens of their own countries. It may be that the economic culture we're creating has less to do with what country we live in than with the economic stratum in which we work. It's up to you to plug yourself into the worldwide group of working people. The risk, of course, is that your next transfer will be to another country. Maybe that sounds exciting to you. Maybe it doesn't. Either way, the more contacts you have, the less likely you are to be passed over if that transfer becomes necessary.

Invoking the Network

If you're like most adults, your job is your main connection with society. If you have a feeling that you may get laid off, that you might be removed from the center of your network, it's time to get moving. Most important, don't let yourself be disconnected from your contacts, even if you're disconnected from your job. Second, if you have reason to think that your job might stop being your main connection with society, start plugging in elsewhere. Maybe it's your children's school. Maybe it's in your place of worship. Maybe it's a garden club. Maybe it's a golf or tennis group. Maybe it's as a volunteer at a nursing home. Maybe it's poker night. What you choose to do isn't as important as choosing to do something. Stay connected with the outside world. As Jan found out, letting a lost job destroy your connection with the world can result in a lonely, even frightening time.

Also, if you see people around you losing their jobs, get your contacts in order. Print out a list of everyone you think could be helpful to you if you need to find another job. But remember that millions of people have been laid off, and they've all been asking their contacts for help. Some executives are beginning to grow weary of colleagues who call only when they need a job. The watershed here is in the kind of relationships you've built with the people on your list. If you've simply assembled a list of contacts to call on if you ever lose your job, your network may not be much use to you. But if you've created relationships in which you brought value and helpfulness to someone else's life, most certainly those people will want to help you in return. If it turns out that you don't need them to help you find another job, fine. But the process of assembling those contacts will have you doing something potentially helpful, rather than simply waiting to see if the ax is going to fall on you.

Finally, if you should lose your job and some of the people in your network treat you differently, don't jump to conclusions about what they're thinking. One of my patients—an older woman whose husband lost his high-powered job—felt ashamed and despondent because her friends hadn't invited them to the latest country club dinner. She assumed her so-called friends didn't feel that she and her husband were worthy of their friendship any more. As we talked about it, I urged her not to make that assumption, not to write her friends off as easily as she thought they were writing her off. She left my office resolved to call them, to try to make that connection again. When I saw her next, she told me how glad she was that she'd called. It turns out that their friends felt guilty and embarrassed that they still had jobs, when they knew her husband worked every bit as hard and as well as they did. Their friends just didn't know how to face them. Remember that people sometimes avoid situations not because they think they're superior to you, but because they simply don't know how to handle them. The reasons you attribute to another person's behavior are rarely entirely accurate.

The most important aspect of networking successfully is the way you approach other people—what you ask and expect of them, what you give to them, how well you learn to interact and cooperate toward the goal of mutual gain. When you get right down to it, networking is about using your people skills to expand your base of support. To do it successfully, you have to be willing to expand someone else's base of support at the same time, and to live by the rule that, in this high-tech world, people skills have become more important than ever.

6

Developing People Power

IT SEEMS LIKE another one of those contradictory truths that people skills should be so important just now. After all, many of us have less contact with people than ever. A growing number of us are working at home, alone or nearly so, connected to our employers and clients by telephone lines and overnight mail. Even in office environments, many of us interact with our computers more than with our office mates. On the surface, it seems that building high-tech skills should be our most pressing goal. And those skills are important. But if you look at it from a mental health viewpoint, it makes sense that personal interactions should, and do, become just as important as technical skills at a time when our working environment is becoming more electronic and less personal. We need each other more than ever. What's more, from a pragmatic viewpoint, the fewer opportunities we have to interact with other people, the more we need to be able to communicate well, respond appropriately, and reinforce relationships with empathy and understanding. We need to make the most of our dwindling opportunities.

Even those of us who still spend the majority of our time working in close contact with other people need ever-improving communication skills. In general, the issues we discuss at work are growing ever more complex. And, these days, we tend to have ever shorter schedules in which to arrive at solutions, make decisions, and get things done. So whether the trend in your job is toward or away from interactions with other people, more than ever, you need people skills.

Don't make the mistake of thinking that "people skills" refers to something superficial—simply a method to get people to do what you want them to do. That couldn't be farther from the truth. People skills have nothing to do with manipulation. The most rewarding interactions with other people spring from empathy and understanding, from valuing others, from genuine care and concern, from working through issues together and reaching a conclusion together, even if that conclusion is an amicable disagreement.

Perhaps it's not so strange after all that, in this time of exploding technology and electronic communication, people skills are more important than ever. It seems natural, somehow, that our trend toward impersonal technology would create an increased desire for the opposite: more softness and contact with people. In fact, I wouldn't be surprised if a whole new group of businesses grow up around that trend—businesses that are highly person-oriented, that provide live people to talk with instead of automated telephone menus, and businesses to whom we'll pay extra because they give us the feeling that we've gone back to the good old days on Main Street, USA. Much of what makes a job meaningful, much of what makes *life* meaningful, is the people we meet and interact with. Even in our multicultural, increasingly global society, where there are so many different ways of living a life, meaningful interactions with other people are crucial. The qualities that mark a good life may differ among cultures, but involvement with other people who care about us is a central component in every culture. Our global expansion has given us more opportunities than ever to interact with and learn from other people. Keeping our interactions joyful and meaningful comes from developing and using people skills.

Someone Else's Shoes

When it comes to relating well with other people, at work or away from work, nothing is more important than a concept commonly known as emotional intelligence. People with emotional intelligence are aware of their feelings and other people's feelings; then they use that awareness to relate well with people, using sound judgment and empathic responses. The simplest way to describe emotional intelligence is as the ability to put yourself in someone else's shoes. It's the ability to pick up a myriad of verbal and nonverbal cues from another person (facial expression, posture, tone of voice, eye contact, and so on) to understand how the person feels in addition to what the person says. It means being able to get outside yourself, become less self-involved, and use your own feelings and experience to connect with what another person is feeling and thinking. Think of a person who makes you feel understood, appreciated, someone who feels with you even if he or she doesn't always agree with you. This person has a high level of emotional intelligence. Usually, you feel safe with a person like this, and your interactions are enjoyable.

Now think of someone who always seems to say the wrong thing—a person who doesn't listen to you, doesn't consider the impact of words before speaking them, and may not care about the impact of words after speaking them. This person has a lower level of emotional intelligence. Interacting with a person like this will probably make you feel frustrated, maybe misunderstood, not heard, possibly offended or hurt at times. You may even feel that the person is intentionally trying to hurt you or exert power over you. The interaction feels difficult and unpleasant; you don't want to do it again any time soon. But if it's a person you work with, you may need to interact every day of the week. You may be required to give or take direction from this person or accept this person's tactless judgments of your work. This person could be your boss.

Above all, in developing your people skills, you don't want to *be* this person. You don't want to routinely and unthinkingly put people off or give them reason to feel that you're out of sync with them or care more about a point of view than you do about them. Here's a good example.

I have a bright and highly educated acquaintance who made plans to drive with a colleague to a formal awards ceremony. The colleague, whose name is Janet, would be taking the stage to accept a very large and important grant. As luck would have it, traffic was heavy and they feared they'd be late. Just before arriving at the event, Janet turned and said, "How do I look?" My acquaintance, whose name is Joe, hesitated for a moment and then replied, "I'm sorry to say this, but that dress makes you look fat." And he was shocked and surprised when Janet burst into tears.

This shows an astonishing lack of people skills, a low emotional intelligence. It has nothing to do with intellect or IQ, because Joe is a very smart and capable man. When I suggested that perhaps he shouldn't have told Janet she looked fat just before arriving at the ceremony, Joe drew himself up and sputtered that honesty was his only policy. He always tells the truth, and the truth was that Janet looked fat. "If she couldn't handle the truth," he proclaimed, "then she shouldn't have asked the question."

This man is losing the forest for the trees. Obviously, telling the truth is generally a good thing to do. It's important to be honest. But there are two crucial people skills here that Joe has missed entirely. One is understanding Janet's motivation for asking her question. It's a process of intuitively internalizing what a person is really asking. Use your life experience and ask yourself what you'd want to hear if you were this person. Janet wanted a boost. She wanted to be buoyed onto the stage by a comment that gave her confidence. She wanted to know if she had spinach in her teeth or if her slip was showing— both of which she could have quickly fixed. She didn't want to know, and didn't need to know, Joe's opinion that she looked fat.

The other people skill that's missing here is an understanding of the relationship between what you say and what the person can do about it. In this case, Janet could do absolutely nothing to address Joe's comment. She couldn't very well change her dress in that instant. But his comment certainly made her wish she could. I'm sure she walked onto the stage two inches shorter than she really was, wanting to disappear under the floorboards. Saying "fat" in that instance did his colleague harm, whereas saying something supportive would have helped her and done no harm to anyone else.

I'm not suggesting that you lie or simply tell people everything they want to hear. Not at all. But take a moment to think about what a person is really asking. Then frame your answer in a way that's constructive.

If you're one of those people who refuses to say anything but what you consider to be the bare-knuckle truth, then ignore the actual question as it was asked and give the person an honest emotional response. That's what Janet wanted in the first place. She couldn't turn to Joe and say, "Tell me something nice about me so I'll feel strong." So she said something much more socially and intuitively understood: "How do I look?" If your conscience won't let you respond positively to that question or a similar one, just skirt it and say something genuine, like, "You're going to be great out there."

Let me add something here about honesty. Some people use honesty—or the Truth—as an excuse for saying any negative thing they want, then washing their hands of the consequences. This is neither honesty nor truth; this is cruelty. Be very careful not to confuse giving your opinion with telling the truth. There are some absolute truths in the world, but personal views rarely fit that category. Don't use your opinions to tear down another person under the guise of being honest. After all, how do you know your views are more correct than someone else's? If you tend to deliver one-two punches and then innocently say you were just being honest, it's time to stop that behavior. It's cruel; if you derive some level of pleasure from the process, it's sadistic.

If you feel you must give someone an opinion that may cause hurt or anger, do two things first. One, put yourself in that person's shoes and think about how you'd like to hear the news. Two, assess your level of concern for that person's feelings. If you *genuinely* care and are concerned about the person, you may be able to find a kind and compassionate way to deliver a negative opinion. Sometimes you have to. But if you don't have that level of care and compassion, I would suggest that you consider keeping your views to yourself if possible. Or at the very least, make it clear that you're delivering an opinion, no more or less likely to be right than the next person's opinion.

Could Joe have expressed his dislike for Janet's outfit and still acted within the bounds of reasonable emotional intelligence? Sure. Given the opportunity, he could have said something two weeks earlier, when Janet was still deciding which dress to buy. He could even have said something after she bought the dress, if he really thought Janet would embarrass herself by wearing it. Even at the time, he could have said something like, "You look like you're ready to go out on that stage and give a great speech." But saying what he said, at the time he said it, showed little emotional intelligence, if any.

Learning Emotional Intelligence

Fortunately, most people can learn to have more emotional intelligence and, consequently, better relationships. People often ask me what would make them more interesting to others, which essentially is asking how to create better relationships. The simple answer is that you become more interesting to other people when you become more interested in *them*. It's a sure-fire way to build relationships, because nothing is more interesting than a genuine interest in other people. Be in tune with them. Try to catch the tone of their emotions. It's not terribly hard. You just have to pay attention and respond in a manner that demonstrates your feelings of understanding and compassion.

If you're watching, you can usually tell how someone is feeling about something, unless the person is deliberately attempting to hide those feelings and is skilled at doing it. Try to read the other person. Try to put yourself in the other person's shoes and feel what the other person feels. This is empathy. Some people have more of an innate ability to be empathic, but we can all learn it.

For example, say you're having a big party for a local dignitary at your house, and your spouse is worried that you don't have enough food. People will be arriving shortly, you're not quite ready, and it's important that this event come off perfectly. Your spouse expresses worries to you about the food shortage and you, thinking you're being funny, say, "Good. Maybe they'll have a lousy time and leave early."

Sometimes you can get away with a response like that and the other person will laugh and lighten up. But it's a risk. In general, if a person is taking something seriously, acting concerned or even worried, and you treat the problem lightly, it doesn't go over well. What you've done is called a failure of empathy—being out of touch with another person's emotional reality as they've expressed it to you. If your spouse or other close friends accuse you of minimizing their issues or problems, they may in fact be giving you clues to your failure of empathy. You're probably doing much the same thing at work, around people who don't know you well enough to say something out loud. Your colleagues may simply go back to their desks feeling that you're difficult and that you just don't get it. You can learn to respond differently.

It's important to be sensitive to the relative urgency or importance of an issue in another person's mind. Even if you disagree, don't mock or lie or scowl or be unresponsive. Respond with empathy. So, for example, if your team leader is agitated over the looming deadline for the Henderson report, say something like, "I understand that this is an urgent problem. From my perspective, though, I have to put it a notch lower on the list than the year-end summary my boss asked me to do. Let's see if we can figure out a way for me to get my year-end summary done and still have time to finish the Henderson report for you." Giving this kind of response accomplishes several goals. First, it gives the team leader the feeling of having been heard. Second, it gives the team leader needed information about competing tasks. Third, it allows you to maintain your goals and priorities. Finally, it expresses a willingness to work together toward a mutually satisfying conclusion.

If it doesn't come naturally to you to adopt another person's frame of reference, work at it. If you care about establishing good relationships, the results will be well worth the effort.

Empathy on the Job

One of the tools that help in learning to apply your empathic powers is taking the time to think before you answer. Remember that the words people use on the surface and the response they want on an emotional level may differ. But the difference is usually discernible if you look for it. Look at the person's facial expression, pay attention to body language. I think of it as the interplay between words and music. While you're hearing the words, don't forget to listen to the music playing under them. This process can help you quickly tune in to what a person is really saying. If you're aware of what someone is thinking or feeling, and you're aware of what you're feeling yourself, you can then react more quickly in an appropriate and understanding way. Just do a little thinking ahead of time. And recognize that today's work environment is creating some intense emotions.

For one thing, be prepared for mature workers (people in their 40s and older) to feel more anxious about our changing environment than younger workers. This isn't the case for every person, but, in general, job loss or the threat of job loss will hit an older worker harder. This happens largely because many of us have grown up thinking of the 20s as a searching time, the 30s as a building time, the 40s as a time to exercise our skills and power, the 50s as a coasting time, and the 60s as the beginning of a resting time. Now imagine the prospect of losing your job at 48 or 50 years old, especially now, when it may be tough to find another job. America's employment practices are forcing middle-aged people back into the tasks of youth, including defining the kind of work they want to do. Understandably, this typically raises feelings of fear and anger. So if you're interacting with workers of varying ages, be prepared to listen and respond compassionately on this topic, especially to employees who are in their 40s and above.

Also be prepared to respond with empathy to people of all ages rocked by confusion over rapid changes in the workplace. Things are changing fast. I had one patient who couldn't remember her boss's name—because the fast-paced software company she worked for had changed her boss eight times in the previous 18 months. By the time she got to boss number eight, she felt incapable of adjusting to yet another set of personal styles and values. The migraine headaches she once got occasionally became more frequent, and more incapacitating. Not everyone will have stresses and reactions this obvious, but the rapid changes we're all going through increase the level of confusion for most people. Most workers are simply not as sharp and focused as they would be in a more stable environment. Try to put yourself in their shoes.

Another tool that can help you learn to apply your empathic skills is a willingness to respect another person's view. We all have different points of view. If you can resist the tendency to turn those views into issues of right and wrong, your empathy will be much easier to find and apply. That doesn't mean you have to fake it or lie or ignore your own views. It does mean, however, that you may not always want to spout your views, depending on your impression of the group you're with. It's not always in your best interest to express your point at all times and with all people. Before you do express a critical viewpoint or opinion, try to find out *why* a person believes something. You may not agree, but at least you'll understand the person a little better. And you'll probably be able to relate with more empathy. You're never going to be able to please everyone, but at least you can make most people feel that they've been heard and respected. Then you can ask for the same treatment in return.

Vive la Différence

These days, it's tough to talk about differences between the sexes without being labeled a sexist. But the fact is that, in a very general way, men and women do have somewhat different tendencies, many of which stem from cultural attitudes, family beliefs, hormone structure, or a combination of all these characteristics. This does not mean that all men are alike or that all women are alike, or that all men exhibit certain traits and all women exhibit different ones. But in a very general way, I believe that you will be best able to engage your empathic skills if you develop some understanding and compassion for the differences between male and female reactions.

Mature women in the workforce today have faced much different emotional pressures than women just now entering the work world. Many women in their 40s and older are conditioned to feel that they must defend their importance—even their existence—in the workplace. When I was in school (Barnard and Columbia, good schools known for their intellectual challenge), I distinctly remember the relative who said to me, "You're not bad looking. Why do you want to go to medical school when you're attractive enough to find a husband?" Later, in medical school, I was told that my presence at that school was keeping a soldier in Vietnam. Comments like these tend to lurk in the emotional underbrush throughout your working life, even if you can usually put them out of your mind or come to see them as superfluous. And although people aren't making comments like that as frequently or as publicly anymore, there's still something of a similar undercurrent.

For example, many supervisors still assume that there's another income in a female employee's home, that a woman doesn't really have to support a family. Many make the opposite assumption about a male employee, even though the vast majority of single parents are women. It's also been my observation that a woman tends to get less sympathy than a man when she loses her job, probably for the same reason. Last but not least, there's still a gap between wages paid to women and wages paid to men, and it has nothing to do with the nature of the work. If you supervise or work with women employees, whether you yourself are male or female, take some time to assess your assumptions about working women, their needs, and the demands on them. Try to understand their reactions to frightening or unfair work situations with this background in mind. Put yourself in their shoes.

Many men, on the other hand, have had the importance of work hammered home so hard that they tend to define themselves by their work. And many left their childhood homes with the mission of a soldier, feeling that they must either march or die—no whining, no crying. Many men still feel responsible to single-handedly provide for a family, even though a hefty portion of the American work force is now female, even though most families now need two wage earners. If a man carrying these messages from his childhood gets laid off, he may feel isolated even from his own family. He may feel like a failure at a considerably deeper level than many women would in similar circumstances. And he may not have any other arena in which to recover his sense of usefulness and purpose.

Even early retirement can be a traumatic event. People around this man will probably think, "Wow, how great! You don't have to work any more. You're free!" But for an executive retiring early and abruptly, without a slow emotional build, this is not the typical reaction. Every aspect of his psychological life may be tied up in his work —his social connections, his sense of power, importance, self-worth. Removing this man's work may be akin to removing the trellis from under a vine. And the closer he is to the top, the farther he has to fall. Even a man who loves his family dearly may feel a profound sense of loss. Suddenly, he's just a regular guy. No more meetings with CEOs, big-budget responsibilities, and efficient secretaries to offer external reminders of his skill and value. In general, men tend to measure their accomplishments by work more than by family. Maybe this is left over from bygone days when women took charge of (and credit for) raising the children. But it still exists. More than women, men need something to do all the time, and something to show for it. So, no matter how financially prepared a man may be for retirement, emotionally, this can be a very difficult time.

If you work with or supervise men who are in their 40s and above, consider the individuals involved. Observe their willingness to express thoughts, feelings, and expectations. Note the differences between men who express themselves freely and those who reveal little. A highly stoic man who says he's worried about the future may, in fact, be much more anxious than an openly expressive man who worries about the future as part of his daily conversation. By paying attention to the differences among people, you'll be better able to measure each man by his own yardstick. You'll be better able to put yourself in his shoes.

Help Yourself

One of the most important sources of people skills comes not from understanding other people, but from understanding yourself—your attitudes, your reactions, your impact on other people. In the workplace, it's common for supervisors and managers to be the *least* in touch with their feelings and emotions. And it's tough to have understanding and empathy for others when you aren't even comfortable with your own feelings. These days, workers are afraid and angry at many desks across this land, and they're reacting, sometimes badly. To many of us, it doesn't seem fair that the employment rules have changed in the middle of the game—that we now have to adapt, like it or not, or we could get kicked off the team. Some workers are angry enough to react in the only way they think they can: by not working. This is called passive-aggressive behavior. It's something like having a temper tantrum. You simply sit down and refuse to get up.

But if you feel this way, and if you act this way, who is your attitude going to hurt? The company president? The board of directors? With whom are you trying to get even? I suspect that your attitude will hurt you much more than it hurts your employer. After all, it quickly becomes apparent who's working and who isn't. Plus, how can you feel good about yourself if you're not trying to do your personal best? When it comes to the quality of your work, it's your reputation on the line, not the company president's.

It's understandable that many of us are angry. But just like all the other beings on earth, we have to keep evolving to suit a changing environment, or we may not survive. Keep in mind that exercise is the best outlet for anger. Go for a walk or a jog. Go to the gym and work out. Get a punching bag and punch it. At the other end of the spectrum, try meditation as another method for releasing anger.

Once you get beyond the hottest part of your anger, the deepest part of your anguish, understand that your moods and attitudes affect the depth and meaning that you can bring to relationships with other people. What's more, understand that your relationships with other people, in turn, greatly affect your moods and attitudes. It's all connected. Everyone has a different level of desire and tolerance for human interaction on a daily basis, but we all need it. A joke told by a friend can lift your spirits and make your situation seem somehow less dire. A sincere compliment can give another person a pleasant and long-lasting surprise. By improving someone else's day, you can improve your own—and feel better about yourself at the same time. Staying connected with the people at work can keep you feeling that you're part of a team, pulling together, doing the best you can in a stormy sea. Other people are going through the same thing you are; maybe they've learned valuable coping skills that you can learn too. Through trying to understand your own emotions, and by putting yourself in the shoes of others, your people skills can become a valuable coping tool.

7

Working with the Wounded

D EVELOPING AND IMPLEMENTING effective people skills
presents a challenge no matter which echelon you occupy
on your company's organizational chart. But if your job includes supervising other people, yours is a special challenge in this
time of rapid and unsettling change. It's up to you to calm not only
your own thoughts and feelings about the changing workplace but
those of the varied people you supervise as well. You have to bolster
sagging morale when your own may not be great. You have to maintain production and quality with a staff who may be caught up in feelings of anger, fear, and confusion. In addition to the difficulties
inherent in any supervisor's job, these days you have to pay closer
attention than ever to the feelings and needs of the people who
report to you: people who may feel jangled, distracted, downright
enraged; people who may tend to see you as the mouthpiece of the
enemy. Some days, your job may feel like quite a struggle.

Being a supervisor or a manager in today's work world is a lot
tougher than it was 10 or 20 years ago. You face new types of pressure, new and unpleasant personnel tasks, and new levels of anxiety
and expectation. You've probably gained a heightened awareness of

the tenuous nature of employment, especially if you're privy to reorganization plans in your company. Your heightened awareness may bring with it a heightened anxiety about your own future. You may have to uphold company policies you don't personally agree with. And if you've had to carry out an order to downsize, or you think you might have to, you may well be battling strong feelings of guilt, anxiety, fear, and anger. Coping with this troubling situation can be difficult at best. No one can give you a potion or prescription to magically make it better. But there's much you can learn from the experience of other supervisors, and much insight to be gained from understanding and applying a few principles of human nature. With courage and compassion, you can help yourself get through this tough time. You can also do much to reduce the distress of people who look to you—their supervisor—for guidance, protection, and trustworthy information.

Difficult Decisions

Picture yourself in the shoes of George Dunlap, a middle-aged, mouse-faced man who supervised production of a cleaning product for a large chemical company. Balding, bespectacled, and bland, George typically wore a sleeveless cardigan over his white shirt and dark tie, to keep from getting cold in his glass-fronted office. Though he brought modest personal warmth to his supervisory position, George's staff had little reason to dislike him—and little reason to seek him out during the day. When the company announced layoffs numbering in the thousands, George could almost feel the fear and anxiety oozing from the people who worked under him. The atmosphere in his department became so palpable that he felt he was walking the halls in a thick, chilly fog. Other supervisors reported widespread distress in their departments as well. After all, theirs was the only big company in town, the major employer and the one real industry. Whoever was unlucky enough to get laid off would find few other options here.

George knew that the reorganization team had targeted his department for reduction, but he didn't know how drastic their recommendations would be. While he waited to hear the news, a steady stream of employees began stopping by his office, leaning against his door frame or standing nervously on the stained carpet across from his desk. Had he heard anything, each one wondered? Did he know what would happen to them? Would jobs be open anywhere else in the company?

To all their questions, George shook his head slowly and said, "I'd tell you if I knew, but I don't know anything." Two weeks after the announcement, George and all the other department supervisors were summoned to the board room. The CEO and CFO sat together at the head of a polished teak table that, to George, seemed long enough to double as a bowling alley. The supervisors sat quietly, churchlike, while the CEO whispered over his shoulder to his officious, widely disliked secretary. George thought he could hear a collective intake of breath at the moment the CEO turned to face the assembled group.

"Ladies and gentlemen," the CEO said smoothly, unruffled, "you know that significant changes are afoot in our business and our industry. These changes have forced us to make some difficult and unpleasant decisions." Has he rehearsed this speech, George wondered, or could he possibly be this casual about what's coming? Moving only his eyes, George glanced quickly sideways at the row of impassive faces. "I want you to know about our decisions well in advance," he continued, "so you'll have plenty of time to assist HR in preparing termination documents for the employees whose positions have been eliminated. I must insist, however, that you keep this information confidential until Friday the eighth, two weeks from today. It's critical that we keep the plant running smoothly and safely until then. If your staff members ask you what's happening, tell them that final decisions haven't been made yet."

With that, the CEO turned to his left and the CFO began listing the numbers of people laid off, department by department. In

George's area, 600 people were slated to go. As the CFO distributed computer printouts listing the names of the doomed in each department, George struggled against his rising anguish. What would these people do? Where would they go? How could he take responsibility for denying them jobs? Why did *he* have to fire them? The anguish only worsened as he walked quickly back to his office, the printout hidden within a manila folder. Small clusters of employees separated into individuals and scuttled back to their places as he approached. Whispered conversations abruptly stopped as he passed. George closed his office door behind him and waited for five o'clock.

Over the next two weeks, George grew more and more anxious about his impending duties. A vice president met with him several times to lay out a plan for George to follow when firing his staff. And whenever an employee waited anxiously, shifting from one foot to the other on his carpet, George found a way to say, "No, I don't know anything yet," a response that has haunted him ever since.

On Friday the eighth, George stopped at a cafe on the way to work and sat staring into his coffee, absently ripping pea-sized pieces of Styrofoam from the rim of his cup until he was 25 minutes late for work. Finally, he carefully brushed the pile of pieces into his nearly empty cup and wedged it in an overflowing trash can on his way out the door. He followed the vice president's plan just as he was supposed to, trying not to think or react to the faces before him, trying not to recognize individuals he had known for years. He imagined this same purge happening simultaneously all over the company. To the several employees who asked how long he had known, George lied.

At the bitter end of the day, exhausted and emotionally undone, George went to his appointment at the vice president's office. Leaning back in a plump chair, George draped his arms along the curve of the upholstery and said softly, "It's done. They're all gone." Expecting to hear vague reassurances and murmurs of appreciation, it took a few beats for George to realize that the man across the desk from him had said, "Don't get too relaxed there George." Suddenly pulled to pinpoint attention, George watched the vice president's thick mustache move as he said, "Now that our ranks are so much thinner, we've decided to reorganize all the departments into three main production units. I'm sorry to tell you that your position didn't make it onto the new plan."

Before George could collect his thoughts, the man picked up the phone and asked his secretary to send the HR director in. Thirty minutes later, George was on the street clutching his briefcase and an umbrella hastily collected from behind his office door.

Strong Feelings

As gruesome and demoralizing as this story may seem, it forces us to recognize the common occurrence of a remarkably difficult situation. People are being laid off by the hundreds of thousands all over the country. Someone has to deliver the news and, usually, it's a supervisor. Emotionally, how do you survive the trauma of having to fire the people who work for you? People you've played touch football with at company picnics. People who've been to your house and met your children. People who've sat in meetings with you assuming that life would continue on its present course. People who've come to know you. People who want to trust you.

There's no way around it. If you care at all about people, you're going to feel terrible. You may be overwhelmed by sadness for a time. You may feel great rage at your company for forcing you to fire basically hard-working, honest people, some of whom may be your friends. You may feel trapped between trying to save your future and trying to save theirs. If you have to fire people, expect to encounter these feelings. Let yourself feel them. Talk with your spouse or a trusted peer or friend about them. If you can, give in to them. You'll feel better sooner if you do.

It's normal to feel these strong emotions in a situation so painful. But there are a couple of feelings you should try to talk yourself out of. They're feelings that won't lead you in a healthy direction. And they won't help the people you're feeling bad about.

First, try not to feel guilty. You can feel sad. You can feel bad for people. But it won't help to feel guilty, as though you've carried out your duties intentionally to hurt them. As long as you work for a company, you're charged with carrying out that company's business to the best of your ability. As a supervisor, you're in a position of authority. You need to understand, and remind yourself, that your mission may differ from that of other employees. You have to do what your employer believes is best for the group, even though it may not seem best for each individual in the group. Your only other option is to resign.

Keep in mind that guilt is a common problem. Many people battle it, not just about work issues but about many aspects of life. If you're a person who battles feelings of guilt, don't be surprised if this difficult work situation aggravates them. But don't let it go too far. If you find yourself weighed down by unrelenting and crippling feelings of guilt over your role in accomplishing a layoff—if you simply can't turn those feelings off—consider talking with a psychiatrist about it. Doing so will provide you with the personalized approach you need to tackle this complex issue.

Second, don't take personally the outrage that may be directed at you from the people who lose their jobs. It's natural that people will feel strong emotions, just like you do. But you shouldn't take on their anger and fear, especially in your role as the messenger. It will hurt you if you do, and it won't help them.

Finally, don't let yourself obsess too much about how this layoff could ruin individual lives. Don't assume you know what's best for people in the long run, or how things ultimately will turn out. Don't assume that a layoff will be the worst thing that's ever happened to these people. You can't possibly predict. And if you let it, your imagination will almost certainly lead you to assume the worst. Entertaining these thoughts and feelings will hurt you, and it won't help the people you're worried about.

Dangerous Denial

Thus far, we've talked about ways to handle the strong feelings many supervisors experience when they're forced to participate in a layoff. But what if you find that you have no feelings about it at all? This is more common than you might think. You're charged with firing some or all of the people who work for you, and you find yourself treating it as one more task on your list of things to do. You just don't seem to feel any human emotion about it. And you may have little empathy for those who do. There are two explanations for a reaction like this. Either you don't care a thing about other people, which probably isn't the case if you're reading this book, or you're in denial of your feelings.

We use this term "in denial" rather frequently in our culture to refer to those people who bury their feelings—consciously or unconsciously—and pretend they don't exist. For some people, denial has become an automatic (although harmful) method for coping with the world. They don't even know they're doing it. The problem, however, is that those feelings *do* exist. People who deny deep emotions have to expend enormous amounts of emotional energy trying not to recognize or feel them. It's hard work to maintain a smokescreen that you don't allow even yourself to see through. And it's pointless, at the end of it all, to have expended all that energy. The fact is that, if you don't recognize and address your feelings, they will come back to haunt you. Unaddressed feelings tend to sneak out in many ways, some of them dangerous and alarming—nervous habits, heart attacks, increased allergies, more frequent illnesses, and inappropriate expression of anger or sadness, for example. Sometimes the absence of feelings in a situation like this one resembles incomplete mourning. If you don't mourn adequately over the loss of someone dear to you, those unaddressed feelings may come back later as chronic depression. You'll learn more about this mind-body connection in chapter 8.

Also, keep in mind that if you numb yourself to feelings of sadness, pain, and grief, you're probably also going to numb yourself to joy, pleasure, and other feelings on the opposite end of the emotional spectrum. Your denial may protect you from feeling some of the lows, but you also won't feel the highs. This seems to be one of the rules that governs emotions: You can't draw back from some emotions without drawing back from all of them.

If you find that you're trying to ignore your feelings about a layoff, acting as though everything is fine when the little voice inside you is telling you the opposite, it's time to change the way you deal with emotions. Recognize that emotions can't be boxed neatly away like knickknacks you no longer want on your living room shelves. In their overall sense, emotions are uncontainable, somewhat messy. That means people can be messy too. We don't fit into neat little emotional compartments the way our names fit neatly into the boxes on an organizational chart. When you're involved in downsizing, underneath it all, you know that you aren't simply deleting boxes from an org chart. You're affecting people's lives and emotions, including your own. Accept it. Embrace it. Be willing to stand in the middle of a storm of emotions—yours and those of the people around you— knowing that you'll be healthier and stronger and more capable if you do. The world would be a boring and joyless place if we deleted emotions from our lives. Let's not try.

If you are one of those people who try to suppress their feelings and act as though everything is fine, you may not want to hear all this. You may not want to hear any of it. It's scary. But believe me, the fear of facing your feelings is worse than actually doing it. Sit down and ask yourself what you really feel about your role in a layoff. Then listen to yourself, and let yourself feel it. Ask yourself what you really feel about the people who will be affected. Then listen to yourself, and let yourself feel it. Try not to engage in those needless, nonproductive feelings you read about earlier in the chapter. And try to contain your reaction to a level that allows you to keep functioning. But, in general, let yourself feel.

Believing Yourself

Some of you are going to be able to accept and implement the advice you've heard thus far, even though your situation is difficult and painful. Others of you will continue to have trouble with it. If you find yourself in the latter category, it may be because you don't believe the reasons you're giving yourself to support your actions on the company's behalf.

We all create a set of constantly evolving reasons, some spoken and some not, to build a logical infrastructure for what we do and believe. This is part of life. It's because, in general, human beings want life to make sense. We want to be able to defend our beliefs—indeed, our existence—with rational, organized thought. Consequently, we construct reasons for virtually everything: why we chose to marry this person, why we belong to that political party, why we drive this car, why we chose that school for the kids. Likewise, in a downsizing or reorganizing situation, you want to give yourself logical reasons for why it's okay to participate in the process. If you don't have those reasons, or if you don't believe the reasons you try to tell yourself, you may not be able to get through the process emotionally intact.

That may be because what you're trying to tell yourself conflicts with what you really believe. Or it may be because firing the people who work for you brings back vague, garbled feelings of childhood dismay linked to loss, cruelty, abandonment, or other traumas. Don't forget that, when it comes to mental functioning, some things happen on the surface (you're aware of them) and some things happen beneath the surface (they're below your level of awareness). The set of reasons we construct to make life seem logical work at a surface level. But there's also a constant stream of activity happening below the surface. If you're having great trouble getting over your role in a downsizing episode, it may be because you're engaged in an internal war between the known and the unknown, the realized and the unrealized, between adult reasoning and childhood emotions, between logical thought and underlying beliefs.

If you don't believe your own reasons, or if you try to convince yourself of something that goes against your underlying value system, your mind and your body may start to revolt. You may have trouble sleeping, develop indigestion, worry excessively, have disturbing dreams. You may start drinking more. You may start eating more, or find yourself unable to eat. The problem here is that people get out of whack when they feel that they're betraying their ethics and beliefs—that underlying set of reasons. Something goes haywire when there's a difference between what you're trying to tell yourself is true and what you really believe is true underneath it all. If you keep pouring your feelings into a holding tank, eventually they're going to overflow and express themselves as mental or physical symptoms.

These relationships and interactions are highly complex, and they're different for each individual. You may not even understand much of what happens beneath your awareness level. But it affects your feelings and reactions just the same. Addressing your feelings may force you to deal with old business you never had to deal with before. And it may lead you to conclude that, for you, there are indeed some logical and acceptable reasons to carry out your employer's intention to downsize.

One logical reason for your role in firing other people is that you are working for the good of the company; it's your responsibility to carry out what they're paying you to do. Another reason for your participation is that the entire company may be threatened if it doesn't reduce the ranks by a certain number. When everyone is threatened with unemployment, downsizing suddenly becomes the lesser of two evils. Each situation may offer its own set of reasons. It's up to you to decide whether you can get behind them or not, whether your logical reasons and your underlying feelings can coexist.

Part of the problem is that many people have trouble knowing what they're really feeling—especially goal-oriented people who go-go-go all day long, taking little time to stop and reflect. Maybe you're one of these people. If you aren't especially in tune with your feelings, listen to your body. Listen to what it's telling you about your feelings. Also listen to the people around you. If two or three people ask if you're okay, or notice that you're irritable or withdrawn, don't dismiss them. Stop and take a few minutes to think about how you're really feeling, and why. Think about the relationships between what you're feeling, thinking, and doing.

Do Something

Even if you can accept and believe your reasons for agreeing to carry out your company's downsizing order, you may still feel pretty lousy about it. If you do, try to find ways to help the people affected by the change. See if you can persuade your company to start an outplacement assistance committee. Find out if the company will invest some money in training people for new jobs. See if the HR department will help laid-off employees construct their résumés. Ask if the company will give laid-off employees access to a few computers and a photocopy machine.

If your company won't help, do something yourself. Volunteer. Give money to your church or a reputable local charity. Start a support group for displaced workers. For particular people, perhaps you can use your own network of connections to help them find new jobs. Do something that will go directly toward helping someone else. Also consider trying to meet with other supervisors who had to fire their employees. Talk with them. Ask them how they coped with the situation, personally and professionally. See if they have helpful ideas you can incorporate at your company. Besides gaining practical suggestions, talking with other people reduces stress and anxiety. It's a catharsis.

You'll also help yourself feel better if you can avoid fuming and fussing over the occasional executive who doesn't seem to be bothered by firing people. There's nothing you can say to make an uncaring person want to care. This person may have a change of heart one day, but you can't make it happen. So don't waste your time stewing about this person. Just think about what you can do to help the people who need it. Also, make sure you're clear about what's inside your realm of ability and responsibility, and what's outside. You can work hard at the former. You'll have to let go of the latter.

If, despite all your efforts, you still find yourself truly miserable, ashamed, and dishonored about having to fire people, you may have to consider leaving the company. Especially if you think the firings will continue, you may have to decide that this job just isn't for you. But try to make a successful transition, so you don't feel that you ran away from an unpleasant job in failure. Consider talking with an objective person—your minister, a mentor, a psychiatrist—to verify that you're making reasonable conclusions about your job and your future. And try to continue functioning to the best of your ability while you're still on the job. Doing so will make you feel good about yourself and keep your integrity intact.

Improving Morale

If you decide to stay at your job and ride out the turbulence, one of your most difficult challenges will be to maintain morale among the employees who are left after a downsizing. This may be especially difficult if those employees tend to think of you as the enemy. Keep in mind that the best place to work is where people feel valued—an extraordinarily difficult feeling to muster in the wake of a layoff. Concentrate on letting your remaining staff know how much you and the company value them, but not in the silly, false ways some companies use. Stay away from happy faces, warm and fuzzy sayings, and superficial morale boosters that require little thought or effort. People can see right through this stuff. Many employees are downright tired of receiving *Good Job!* stickers when they feel as if the company is falling down around them. Wouldn't you be?

Don't underestimate the intelligence or the intuitive skills possessed by the people who work for you, no matter what jobs they perform. People are not stupid. In general, they can tell when you're tying to dupe them or get away with something. They can smell a patronizing attitude a mile off. So be genuine. Give your staff as much information as you can. Admit that you thought the downsizing was awful too, that it's not easy for anyone involved. Tell your staff honestly when you think they've done a good job. Give compliments specific to the person receiving them. Demonstrate that you trust and have confidence in the people working for you, especially in these stress-filled times. If they want flex time and you think it would be good for them and for the company, try to get the company to adopt it. If they want a casual-dress day and you think it fits within the company's goals, try to make it happen. If another shake-up is on the way, urge the executives to be as forthcoming as possible, and tell your staff that you've done so. You're their team leader, after all. The least you can do is include them on the company's team.

Watch Out

Remember that people are going to express reaction to a layoff in many different ways. Some people will express anger and cynicism. Some may be nearly paralyzed by anxiety. Some may try to get even. Some may try to overcome their fear of being fired by any means possible, including behaving badly enough to force that very outcome. You may see other problem behaviors as well.

Watch carefully for signs of blaming, scapegoating, and revenge against the company. Be aware that some people tend to adopt an "I'll get you before you get me" attitude. They may be tempted to steal things—supplies or ideas—or they could work to subvert other members of your staff. This is passive-aggressive behavior. Keep in mind, however, that the number of people who actually adopt this philosophy is much smaller than most company executives fear. Be careful not to treat good people like criminals.

Also, watch for people who begin to show signs of self-destructing. We all do self-destructive things from time to time, especially when we're under stress. When people see coworkers losing jobs, it's natural that they should fear for their own as well. If this fear becomes uncomfortable enough, if the out–of–control feelings become too intense, a small number of your employees may unconsciously try to regain that lost sense of control in a negative and self-destructive way: by forcing you to fire them. These are the people who become obstinate, lazy, and argumentative instead of working more diligently in an effort to keep their jobs. If you encounter someone like this on your staff, try to avoid coming down hard. That's just what the person feared would happen and only reinforces the tendency. Instead, try to talk with the person, gently and honestly. You can't try to be a shrink. But you can talk about the behaviors affecting this person's performance. Try to get the person to talk about the real feelings buried somewhere under the hard–edged surface. Try to reach agreements that help both of you feel some control. You may not get anywhere, but the person will leave your office knowing, on some level, that you cared enough to try.

The bottom line is that we each have the responsibility for our own lives. You can't save people if they don't want to be saved. And you have to remember that you're a boss, not a mental health expert. But you can still try to relate with people who work for you in a caring and empathic manner. They'll feel better about you and the company you represent, and you'll feel better about yourself for trying.

Finally, be aware that many people who survive the layoff tend to feel guilty about it. Why did my coworkers get fired and I didn't? Did I do something sneaky or bad to keep my job? These people will keep working, but they may feel that they're working at the expense of others who were just as competent, experienced, and worthy as they are. They may wonder, "Why me?" This feeling is called survivor guilt, and it first came to light after the German death camps were liberated. Survivors suffered debilitating guilt that they lived while so many others did not. On a smaller scale, employees may feel a similar guilt that they survived while others did not.

People with survivor guilt may have an increased tendency to undermine themselves or do self-destructive things. They may lose motivation or the willingness to take a risk or accept a challenge.

They may try to find security by vigorously supporting—even identifying with—executives who ordered the layoff. They may even worry that their wish to keep a job *caused* other people to be fired. If you have reason to believe that someone's performance is suffering because of survivor guilt, try to find a way to talk about it. If it's true, tell the person that people were selected for layoff randomly. If that's not true, get to the real point: Giving up your job or doing it badly will not bring back the people who got laid off. It will hurt you and it won't help them. Feeling guilty won't help either. Perhaps you survived on your own merit. Maybe you argue less than other employees. Maybe you work more effectively. Or maybe your face reminds the vice president of his best friend from high school. Maybe you're better at what you do; maybe you're just lucky; maybe it's a combination of both. For whatever reason, you still have your job. The only reasonable course of action is to respect yourself and do your job well.

If you can communicate these concepts clearly, you may be able to help people let go of a responsibility they don't have and events they can't influence. We all have to find ways to resolve the things that weigh heavy on our consciences. Above all else in your position as a supervisor, don't do things that will make you feel diminished, less decent in your own eyes when you look back on them months or years later. It's partly a matter of setting boundaries, as we discussed in chapter 4. If you find ways to accomplish your job within the bounds of your own ethics and beliefs, you'll increase your chance of surviving a layoff with your self-respect intact. And you'll increase the chance that your employees will as well.

PART II

Pink Slip Blues

8

Call It a Feeling

I F YOU LIVE IN CALIFORNIA, you realize, somewhere in the back of your mind, that one day an earthquake could level your home. If you live in Kansas, you scan the summer sky for tornadoes. If you live in Florida or the Carolinas, you brace for hurricanes. But no matter how much you try, there's no way to prepare yourself fully for the day the roof caves in. The event itself still leaves you stricken, lost, laden with grief. Knowing that you face a heightened risk of disaster doesn't seem to help a great deal when the disaster comes knocking at your front door.

Such is the situation for American workers. We know what's happening in the workplace. We see the television coverage and read the newspaper reports of companies big and small cutting legions of workers adrift from their jobs. But while being mentally prepared can help you survive in many practical ways, it probably will not spare you from the range of emotions that arise as a result of the event. Even if you see a layoff coming, emotionally, it may still knock you flat.

This isn't necessarily true for everyone. A lucky few may be able to see a layoff as an opportunity right away. But usually, these are the people who know what they'll be doing next—people who retain an ample revenue stream despite the loss of a job, people who have several months' salary stashed in a liquid account, people who were already detaching from their previous jobs, people who may not have been attached in the first place. Keep in mind, however, that even these people still need to cope with a substantial change in their lives. And frankly, my observation is that it's unusual to sail through a layoff with no emotional repercussions.

The real variable in this equation is the severity of those repercussions—how long they last and how deeply they cut. It's here, with this variable, that you can have some influence on your present and your future. By recognizing and facing your feelings, and working through them in a healthy way, you can find ways to mitigate their impact and get on with your life.

Emotional Crisis

Loss of your job is an emotional crisis to which you are bound to have a reaction. For some people, the reaction is severe. For others, it's mild. But in general, it's unusual not to feel bad if your job is taken away from you. Expect it. When you lose a job, you lose a social network, a source of economic security. Particularly in our country, you lose a common mechanism for describing your purpose and identity in the world. It may feel as though you're no longer needed, no longer worthy, that you don't have a place to fit.

The severity of your reaction—how hard the loss of your job hits you, and how long those feelings last—depends on a number of factors like these, not necessarily in this order:

- Your age
- How long you've worked for the company you're leaving and how long you've held the specific job you're losing
- How surprised you are by the layoff
- The extent to which your identity is wrapped up in your job
- How easily you can make the transition into a new and satisfying job

- How long you expected to keep the job you're losing
- How strapped you are financially
- Your level of coping skills, self-esteem, and general mental health
- Your physical health
- Other stressful situations taking place in your life at the same time
- The net effect of the people in your life

Based on these and other circumstances and characteristics, your reaction to a layoff may range from a few days of feeling dislocated and sad to months or years of debilitating grief, anger, and guilt. Most people find themselves somewhere in the middle. The common denominator is that, if you invest anything of yourself in your job, you're going to have a reaction. Remember how bad it felt when you got rejected after a first date? Didn't get picked for the team? Didn't get the promotion you thought you deserved? How could you not react to what feels like personal rejection by the people you work for, people who presumably know you pretty well, people who hold the reins to a large portion of your self-esteem? It's okay to react.

Think of it like this. When someone loses a loved one, the period of time spent in bereavement is usually about six months, maybe longer. It's similar for a divorce. For some people, the loss of a job they've held for many years (especially a job with a big firm where employment was supposed to last forever) may involve a grieving process just as intense. Don't try to decide whether it *should* or not. Just let it be whatever it is. It makes sense, doesn't it? After all, where do you spend most of your time? Where do you expend the majority of your effort? For most of us, it's on the job. It's not so odd to think that a layoff would result in a grief reaction similar to what you'd experience after a death or divorce. It may, in fact, be a loss of similar magnitude.

Wherever you find yourself on the yardstick of emotional reactions to a layoff, I offer the same initial advice. Let yourself feel. Whether you're worried about being laid off, planning to be laid off, or have already been laid off, recognizing and naming your feelings gives you some power over them. This doesn't mean you can let your feelings take over. You should be able to put them aside temporarily so you can function in a relatively normal way. But in general, don't ignore your feelings. Doing so will only prolong the time you'll need to work through them. And eventually, you *will* need to work through them if you want to get on with a healthy life.

Mind and Body

The first step in working through your feelings is to identify them. In general, a layoff can produce a wide variety of thoughts and emotions. You may feel a sense of grief and sadness, a feeling of loss, a need to mourn. You may experience denial, where you tell yourself that this can't really be happening. You may find yourself going over and over in your mind what you could have done differently, asking yourself if it was your fault, if your performance on the job was defective somehow. You may feel guilty that you didn't do enough to keep your job, guilty that you didn't save enough money to support yourself and your family while you look for another job. Your feelings of guilt may alternate with feelings of betrayal. You may find yourself focusing blame for your layoff on a particular person or group of people. You may be anxious about what the future will hold, and whether or not things will work out for you. You may feel out of control. You may even experience occasional periods of extreme anxiety. You may have trouble sleeping at night. You may find yourself drinking more than usual. Your eating habits may change. You may feel anger, possibly a lot of anger, bordering at times on rage. If you still have to work at your job for a while before the layoff takes effect, you may have trouble functioning at your usual level. You may find yourself agitated and snappish, or unusually slow and distracted. These feelings and behaviors may occur at different times, or they may superimpose on each other.

It's easy to see how losing your job can be an enormous stress on your mind. But don't forget that your mind and body are intimately connected. In fact, the mind-body connection has been well documented over the years. So don't be surprised if physical effects arise as a result of your emotional stress level. And don't be afraid to think of these physical and emotional reactions as being linked to one another.

The kind of physical reactions you display will probably depend in part on how your body typically expresses its vulnerability. If you tend to get headaches, the added stress will probably make them worse. If you tend to have an irritable digestive system, it may accelerate into a spastic colon or peptic ulcer disease. If your vulnerability is in your skin, you may break out, peel, or get dandruff. If you have a skin condition, it may get worse. If you have asthma, you may become more susceptible to attacks. If you have high blood pressure, it may get higher. If you have heart disease, you may face an increased risk of angina or heart attack. Aside from problems you already know about, physical reactions may surface in areas that never bothered you before. These, too, may be related to your emotional state. Plus, your immune system may be affected. You could develop an increased susceptibility to viral infections, such as a cold or the flu. You may feel fatigued. This complex set of reactions occurs because of the intimate connection between your mind and your body.

Not only will a layoff affect your mind and body, it may affect your relationships as well. I'll talk in detail about this topic later in the book. In the meantime, however, keep in mind that your mood can greatly affect the moods of the people around you, and vice versa. If you're feeling anxious or depressed, your friends and loved ones may react to it or succumb to it. If you're sad or dejected, your interest in sex may decline—a change your mate may tend to take personally. If you spend your day on the couch while your spouse gets dressed and goes off to work, feelings of resentment may creep up in one or both of you. And if your emotions are more volatile than usual, you may find more tears and anger marking your interactions with loved ones.

Last but not least, there are practical issues to worry over. How will you pay the bills? Are you in danger of losing the house? Will you have to work two or three minimum wage jobs to survive? Will your lifestyle have to change dramatically?

Trying to Cope

By now it's obvious that a layoff can affect every area of your life: emotional, physical, relational, financial. What can you do to help yourself get through this difficult time relatively intact? If possible, do as much as you can to ease the blow before it lands. If you see people getting laid off around you, or you know your company is facing reorganization, it does help to prepare, even though preparation alone won't spare you from an emotional reaction. Make sure you're paying attention to the principles outlined in the first part of this book. And put some money aside, as much as you can. It may be worth going without a few things while your paychecks are still coming in, so you'll have something to live on if your paychecks stop. The good news is that, if the paychecks don't stop, you'll have some savings to rely on if the situation arises again in the future.

Also, although this may sound minor at first, try to get enough sleep. Sleep deprivation weakens your coping skills. Chronic lack of sleep can make you more agitated and irrational than you would ordinarily be. It also renders you less able to use your adaptive skills successfully. The same applies to drinking too much, getting no exercise, and eating a poor diet. Remember, the way you care for your physical body will be reflected in your body's capacity—and your mind's ability—to deal with the things that are stressful for you.

In dealing with emotions raised by a layoff, keep in mind that it's important not to personalize too much. Don't lose sight of the big picture. People are being downsized all over the place, from corporate officers to custodians, and everyone in between. Usually, mass layoffs are based on strategic business decisions, not personal issues that have to do with who you are or the quality or speed of your work. The vast majority of the time, it's not personal. It's okay to feel like a victim a little bit because, in reality, we're all victims of a rapidly changing business environment. But don't take the victim role too far. Don't personalize it too much or single yourself out for special victim status. It won't help you get back on your feet, and it won't help you maintain your self-respect or the respect of the people around you—including the people interviewing you for your next job.

Finally, try not to play the "if only" game with yourself. It will not help you. Many people fall into a pattern of berating themselves with "if only" statements: If only I had worked harder, I might not have lost my job. If only I had realized the company was going to downsize, I might have been able to find another job sooner. If only I had been a better provider, we might have more savings to rely on. If only I had finished my degree, it might have been easier for me to find another job. While it's valuable to reflect on your actions and their results, punishing yourself by agonizing over "if only" statements simply wastes your mental and physical energy. And at a time like this, you need all your mental and physical energy working for you, not against you.

If you're laid off from your job, you may feel at first as though you've been hit by a truck. But this feeling will diminish over time. Your life is going to move on. This event doesn't have to cause permanent damage. Do what you can to maintain your mental and physical health and your positive outlook on life. Keep in mind that you still have everything you came into your job with, probably more if you learned new things and met new people while you worked there. If you allow yourself to feel, allow yourself to grieve, and try to maintain supportive relationships through it all, before long you'll find yourself looking toward the future instead of concentrating on the past. And although no one would choose to be laid off, you may find that you're a stronger person as a result of it—a person who can eventually gain confidence and self-esteem by making it through this difficult period.

A Dark Place

For most people, the emotional trauma following a layoff gradually dissipates. You simply wake up one morning feeling better. You begin to notice and appreciate the world around you again. Your place in that world seems more assured. You feel that you can handle it, whatever it is. Your focus leaves the source of your emotional pain and shifts to questions like, "What should I do now? What options do I have? What's the best way for me to move forward?" For some people, however, the loss of a job—especially if combined with other difficult emotional conditions—can bring on a darker, deeper reaction that doesn't seem to lift. If it lasts long enough, and it affects your usual level of functioning seriously enough, you may be in an acute or chronic depressive state, what doctors call a clinical depression or a major depressive episode.

Many people say they're depressed when they experience a day or two of feeling down in the dumps or sad, but this is not clinical depression. It's quite normal to feel sad sometimes, to have the blues or feel for a little while that life is a drag. That's nothing to worry about, and, in fact, it may give you a valuable opportunity for reflection, quietness, and redirection in your life. Clinical depression, on the other hand, is a serious mental disorder suffered by millions of people each year in the United States alone. The condition may last months or years without treatment, and, unattended, it could alter the rest of your life.

How do you know if you have clinical depression? Here are some of the more common symptoms.

- You feel depressed, helpless, and hopeless.
- You don't care about the things that usually interest you, such as hobbies, friends, sex, work.
- Your dietary pattern changes. You may lose your appetite, or you may find yourself eating too much and gaining weight.
- Your sleep is disturbed. You may sleep all the time. You may awaken before dawn and have trouble going back to sleep. Or you may have trouble sleeping at all.
- You're slowed down, or possibly agitated and restless.
- You feel constantly fatigued, so that any small movement takes a major effort.
- You constantly criticize yourself for things that happened in the past or things that are happening now.

- You have difficulty concentrating or making decisions.
- You may find yourself wondering if life is really worth living.

If you have five or more of these symptoms (especially the first two) and they last nearly all day, every day, for more than about two weeks, you may have entered a clinical depression. And if, after that two weeks or so, you seem to be staying the same or getting worse instead of getting better, it's time to seek some treatment. The longer you sit at home surrounded by your dark thoughts and feelings, the more you lose your frame of reference and your grasp of reality. Some people wait months or years before getting help, and then wonder why they did. If you feel immobilized, despondent, unable to rouse yourself toward feeling better, if you find yourself inching toward thoughts of suicide, please don't wait any longer. It may seem like a monumental effort to get yourself some assistance. So if you can't make yourself do it, tell someone in your family that you want help. You'll find that you have resources at hand to help you get through this dark time and get back on the road to feeling better.

By the way, if you're one of those family members to whom a depressed person expresses a need for help, don't wait. Don't ignore it. Don't hope it will go away on its own. Take the action that your loved one can't muster. You've been given the ball. Now run with it. Find a good psychiatrist, explain the situation as clearly as you can, and take the first available appointment. If you have to wait too long for an appointment, ask for a referral to another good doctor who might have an appointment open sooner.

You probably know that there are lots of different mental health professionals to choose from. I recommend going first to a psychiatrist because this type of doctor is trained to diagnose and treat mental *and* physical disorders, using psychotherapy and medications in varying combinations, as needed. Psychiatrists go to medical school, just as family doctors do. Plus, they get several more years of intensive training in diagnosing and treating mental health issues. This means that psychiatrists are prepared to understand all aspects of mental and physical health. It may turn out that the psychiatrist eventually refers you to another type of mental health professional (or to your family doctor for a physical). But especially in the beginning, I think your best bet is with a doctor who can use the full range of diagnostic and treatment options.

Overcoming Obstacles

One of the difficult aspects of a situation like this one is finding the good doctor that you need. How do you know if a mental health professional is good or not? There's no surefire way. But if several people, several different sources, give you the same name, that's a good indication. If you live near a university or a teaching hospital, a well-respected medical institution, call a professor or a department head and ask for a recommendation. If you live near a community hospital, call the staff office and ask who they'd recommend. If you think your family doctor is sensitive to mental health issues, ask that doctor for a referral suggestion. Or you can call your local mental health association. Keep in mind that the person may want a brief description of the patient's problem before making a recommendation. If you belong to a managed health care plan and you want your insurance to cover it, be sure to have a list of the plan's mental health providers with you when you call for a recommendation. If you want more information about the doctor (or doctors) recommended to you, you can order a report that lists the doctor's background and qualifications. Go to the Resources and Readings section in the back of the book for more information about this service.

Another difficult aspect of this situation is the reluctance many people feel about going to see a psychiatrist at all. I can't tell you the number of people who've told me that they don't want to see a shrink because they're not crazy. I make a point of asking each one what crazy means. We all use the word in everyday speech. But "crazy" doesn't have an entry in the official reference book that describes mental health disorders. Psychiatrists don't think in terms of patients being crazy or not. We simply think of *people* and what they need to feel better and function better. We're doctors who believe that mental disorders can be diagnosed, treated, and improved. So don't worry about whether you're crazy or not. That's not the issue. Try to think of mental health as a bell-shaped curve. Most people fit within a certain band of thoughts and behaviors that we've come to consider "normal." Most of the people who seek mental health treatment are within this band. But you may find yourself in different places on the curve at different times of your life. That's nothing to be overly worried about. Just take care of yourself; get the care your mind and body (including your brain) need to feel better.

While you don't need to hide the fact that you're getting mental health care, you also don't need to feel obligated to tell anyone you aren't comfortable telling. This is your private life, after all. You just need to know in your own mind that there's no need to be embarrassed about seeing a psychiatrist. The brain is an organ, just as your heart and your stomach and your thyroid are organs. The brain is made up of cells and chemicals, just like the rest of your body. If you have a heart problem, are you embarrassed to go to the doctor? Of course not. You go as soon as you can get in. If you have a thyroid problem, are you ashamed to have it treated? No. You can't wait to feel better. Why is your brain any different? Of course I know the answer to this question, but the answer is misguided. Your brain is the seat of your spirit, your mind, your soul, if you will. So the reason you're embarrassed to see a psychiatrist is that it feels as if there's something wrong not with your body, but with "you"—something wrong with who you are, maybe something that you should be able to fix by yourself. But many times, when someone has a major depressive episode, the chemicals in that person's brain have gotten out of alignment. It simply isn't something you can fix by yourself.

The human brain contains about 12 billion nerve cells and receives more than 100 million nerve messages from your senses each second. Messages are transmitted to your brain and within your brain by jumping from one nerve cell to the next. That jump is accomplished by chemicals that carry the message along. I sometimes call those chemicals neurohormones to help people understand them; officially, they're known as neurotransmitters. When those chemicals are out of balance, sometimes we can observe that imbalance as a change in the person's mental state.

It's fortunate that we don't feel about all the body's chemicals the way we do about brain chemicals. If you're low on insulin, as in diabetes, you go to the doctor and get a prescription for it. If your thyroid isn't producing enough of the hormones it's supposed to, or if it's producing too much, you get it fixed. If you contract pneumonia, you take medication to get better. You don't say, "No, doc, I can figure this out on my own. I don't need medicine." That's absurd. And while it's true that thoughts and behaviors are more complex than chemical balance alone, I would suggest that we start thinking more like this—in a more scientific, more rational way—about the brain and the chemicals it produces. If we do, we'll start to remove some of the stigma from mental health care and make it more parallel to other kinds of health care: a means of detecting and easing health problems.

A third difficulty in getting treatment for a mental health condition may be financial. Many health plans these days offer only a limited amount of mental health coverage, if they offer any at all. But please don't make the mistake of thinking that, just because your health plan doesn't cover something, you can't have it. If you think going to a psychiatrist will help you, go. Pay for it yourself if your insurance won't cover it.

Getting good mental health care, if you need it, is a very good investment because nothing is as precious as your mental and physical health. If you don't get the care you need, you could be risking your ability to work, to make decisions, to relate to others, even to exist. Think of all the money we spend on making ourselves and our homes and our cars and our yards—our surroundings—look good. How much more important is it to invest what you need to invest in helping yourself and your loved ones feel well and function well? How you perceive the world and yourself in that world is more important than anything material. If you can invest in a course of therapy that prevents you from damaging your career, your reputation, your marriage, your life, and your children's lives, take out a loan if you have to, and get the therapy. Don't let insurance—or the lack of it—stop you.

Brain Changes

As you begin to develop a relationship with the doctor of your choice, there are a couple of ideas that you should try to keep in mind. They'll help your doctor help you. And they'll help you help yourself.

In therapy, there are two important keys to successfully changing your thoughts and behavior. First, you have to want to change. No amount of pushing or prodding can make someone change if they don't want to, even in a psychiatrist's office. And second, you have to have courage. Let me be more specific about that word courage. Many people think of courage as a kind of unfettered bravery, a brazen confidence that defeat is impossible, a swaggering, superhero kind of trait. No. That's not right. Courage is about overcoming fears. In fact, there is no such thing as courage without fear. Think about it. If you aren't afraid of something, there's no need for courage to overcome it. In my view, courage is what I see my patients exhibit all the time, when they struggle against themselves, outside the bounds of their comfort zones, on the road to becoming the people they know they want to be. This is hard work. It requires thoughtfulness and repetition and commitment. It demands a willingness to enter the unknown and try something new. Sometimes it's downright frightening. The good news about courage is that anyone can have it. You don't have to be a superhero. You have to be much more real than that.

If you're in a clinical depression, the subject of medication may come up in addition to psychotherapy. This is another area where many people feel uncomfortable, an area where the word "crazy" tends to rear its head again. And once again, I'll remind you that the brain is made up of cells and chemicals, just like other organs in the body. If those chemicals are out of balance, taking a drug to help put them back in balance is no different from taking insulin or a synthetic thyroid hormone. There should be no value judgment here. It's simply a medication that can help restore your mental health. Like other medications, mental health medications can be overused or underused. But when they're prescribed appropriately, their effect can make the difference between functioning and not functioning, enjoying and not enjoying, and, in some cases, living and not living.

There's no reason to suffer longer than you need to simply because you're uncomfortable about taking the medication that would make you feel better. I know a doctor who experienced a depression severe enough to require hospitalization. Officials at the institution he entered believed in using only psychotherapy, so he got no medication. He stayed there for three months, and he was virtually as depressed on the day he left as on the day he entered. Then he went to his local psychiatrist, who prescribed the medication he needed. Within the month, he was back at work and on the way to a complete recovery. The moral of the medication story is this: If you don't need a medication, don't take it. If you do need a medication, do take it. In both cases, you'll help yourself back to health more effectively. If you aren't sure about something your doctor has prescribed for you, get a second opinion before you take it. If the second opinion doesn't agree with the first, get a third opinion. You have a choice about the medications you take, and it ought to be an informed choice. It's important to feel confident that you need and will benefit from a medication prescribed for you.

Finding a Balance

Mental health medications are getting better all the time. Doctors now have several classes of medications to choose from, all of which are quite effective, although they differ in their specificity. The newer ones have fewer side effects than ever. And researchers believe that, within the next decade, they'll be able to customize medications for treating various kinds of depression. How will they do that? In simple terms, they'll do it by targeting the medication to work on specific chemicals that transmit electrical impulses between nerve cells in the brain. These are the chemicals that get out of balance in some kinds of mental illness. We can alter the balance of these chemicals with medications right now. But in the future, medications promise to become even more fine-tuned.

By improving the chemical balance in the brain, medications can improve the way you think about yourself and your life. This is a fascinating, almost miraculous, concept. An equally interesting concept that we can also apply right now is its reciprocal: To a limited extent, you can influence the balance of chemicals in your own brain by what you think. It is literally true that what you think about yourself affects how you feel about yourself. How you think and what you think can alter what's happening in your brain. Likewise, what's happening in your brain can affect how and what you think. This phenomenon is called a feedback loop. It's all connected and, in fact, forms the basis of a concept called cognitive therapy. Cognitive therapy teaches you to become aware of how and what you think. Then it helps you modify your thinking patterns, changing the balance of chemicals in your brain in the process.

In a very general and simplified sense, the chemical influence works like this. When you are anxious, angry, or frightened, your body produces adrenalin and some other related hormones. This extra burst of adrenalin would be very handy if a tiger were chasing you and you had to run quickly away and climb up a tree to save yourself. But even though we don't typically get chased by tigers in this day and age, those hormones continue to pour out in response to anxiety, anger, and fear—emotions that your body reacts to as though you were facing an external threat, like a tiger.

In essence, these emotions signal the body that you are under attack, and your body responds with an outpouring of fight-or-flight hormones. But if you're anxious and angry and fearful about work or being laid off from work, there's nothing to fight and nothing from which to flee. You simply have to deal with these aggression hormones circulating in your body. In a way, they can wear your body out. This constant, keyed up, fight-or-flight status is not to your benefit. It burns up all your energy on nothing more than making you weary. So what can you do to reduce those fight-or-flight hormones if you don't have a tiger to run away from? The healthiest and most effective solution is exercise. You may not be running and climbing a tree, but you can work through the adrenalin just the same on a racquetball or tennis court, walking, jogging, doing yoga, or whatever else you choose. Just get moving.

Meditation is another good option because it cuts down on production of adrenalin and associated hormones. Find ways to help yourself be calm and serene. Help yourself think positive, optimistic thoughts. If that's hard for you, hang out with positive, optimistic people. I can guarantee that, if you're open to it, their attitudes will rub off on you. Also, find plenty of reasons to make yourself laugh. It's a great way to help change your levels of anxiety and anger. It's also a great way to help yourself conserve energy for more constructive pursuits, like getting over the emotional aftermath of a layoff.

Keep in mind that this phenomenon doesn't apply only to fight-or-flight urges. It applies to all thoughts and emotions. If you tend to be sad, you can modify that tendency through the things you tell yourself and the things you do. The very act of smiling releases chemicals that can help you feel less sad. If you tend to be pessimistic, you can modify that tendency. The theory applies in a general sense: You can modify the thoughts and feelings you carry in your brain.

Get Moving

Once you recognize and accept the fact that a layoff can produce some strong feelings, you can move on to the next thought: There are plenty of healthy and helpful ways to address and work through those feelings. While you're navigating this working-through process, or any time of major stress or change in your life, try not to make any major decisions, like getting a divorce, running away to the south of France, jumping off a bridge, or resuming a drinking habit. If you can, just try to maintain while you process through your feelings. If you don't have a person to talk to about it, find someone you can trust—a parent, sibling, spouse, friend, mentor, pastor, laid-off peer, or mental health professional. Find someone who can give you the respect and support you deserve in what can be a difficult emotional time. By doing so, you can start yourself back on the road to being the kind of person you want to be.

9

Assess for Success

IN MOST CASES these days, getting laid off has little or nothing to do with the kind of person you are or the caliber of work you do. More often than not, today's layoffs result from strategic business decisions. They're part of an effort by company executives to spur business on toward greater and greater success. To help speed their goal, nearly everyone has adopted a take-no-prisoners philosophy. So you may find yourself left by the side of the road while your company continues in another direction without you. This is not personal. Most likely, you were simply in the wrong place at the wrong time in the century.

This is the reality of our economy right now. We're in a time of incredible change. But massive changes have happened in earlier times. And they'll probably happen again, in a future age and in an unheralded way. Imagine the agricultural workers born at the time of the Industrial Revolution. It wasn't their fault that the nation evolved toward industrialization. And it didn't happen because family farmers were doing a bad job. Most of the displaced farmers were probably doing a great job and working hard at doing even better. But they lost their dominant place in the economy anyway, because the economy changed around them.

While the loss of your job feels like a very personal blow, it's important to try to consider it in its sociocultural context. What's going

on around you? What's happening to other workers in your field? What's happening to other workers nationwide? Worldwide? For America, the answer is clear. Everything is shifting. The labor supply is moving offshore. The thrust of our economy is changing. The developing world is hot on our heels. Corporate leaders have adopted a new paradigm of success. No one knows how it ultimately will turn out for workers.

What you can know, however, is that in this time when our economic world is swirling and turbulent, you can rest assured that the loss of your job probably has little direct relation to your personal performance. It's not your fault.

But wait. Here's another one of those contradictory truths. While losing your job these days probably isn't your fault, it is your responsibility. It's your responsibility to work toward being the person you want to be. It's your responsibility to try to make sure your layoff really wasn't rooted in your performance or your personality. If it was, it's your responsibility to address those issues and to make yourself the kind of adaptable, resourceful, employable person who can find a good job even in a time of downsizing. I believe that this is not only possible but mandatory for mental health and professional success. For ourselves and the sake of our loved ones, our communities, and our nation, we must adopt a philosophy of personal responsibility. I realize this may seem hard to do at a time when many of us feel victimized by the profit-minded practices of corporate America. But it's the only way out of our maze of anger and fear. I've seen many people start this journey toward personal responsibility in the past 25 years. And I can tell you without reservation that it's a journey toward increased personal strength and satisfaction. Consider what happened to Jerry Richards, for example.

Getting Ahead

Jerry first came to see me when he was in his mid-20s. Wearing a button-down shirt and khaki pants, blond hair scooped low over one eye, he looked like the all-American guy next door. But Jerry was a quiet and serious young man. Over the course of several visits, he haltingly described to me a frightening and demoralizing childhood with an alcoholic father and a chronically depressed mother. Understandably, he too was mildly but chronically depressed (a condition called dysthymia) and somewhat prone to panic attacks. In college, Jerry studied cellular biology and, after graduation, went to work for an upstart high-tech laboratory. He worked there for the first three years I knew him.

Jerry described himself as a methodical and careful worker. He tended to his work, and he did well at his job. A few months after Jerry was hired, his company celebrated the launch of a new and potentially lucrative product that allowed patients to test at home—at a fraction the cost—what once had required a visit to the doctor's office. It was the high point of his young company's existence. But two years later, that existence seemed threatened by a brewing class-action suit and a firestorm of negative publicity. While the young executives struggled to save their company from bankruptcy, Jerry and the other employees struggled over the course of their futures.

Jerry, for one, suffered a renewed surge of panic attacks, not so much because he feared losing his job, but simply because he didn't know what would happen. Nothing was resolved. No one knew what to do. Everything seemed at loose ends. But Jerry had a couple of things going for him: his age and his expectations. At 28 years old, Jerry had grown up believing that employment is rarely permanent. He didn't expect to work for the same company until retirement. So with the help of continued psychotherapy and medication to reduce his anxiety, Jerry began to tie down, for himself, some of those frightening loose ends.

Jerry started by investigating his options. He asked acquaintances in his industry what they'd heard about his company's prognosis. He went to all the in-house status meetings, where company lawyers discussed the impending litigation. He brought his resume up to date and had it printed on attractive paper. And although he didn't know whether he'd actually leave his company or not, he did start asking around—in person and on the Internet—to see if jobs were coming open at other companies. Lo and behold, he found a few. And one of them was a perfect fit.

It turns out that a competing high-tech company was looking for a technician who knew how to navigate the Net. Executives there wanted to create a new position devoted to developing and running an online system for communicating laboratory data to doctors, health care companies, pharmacies, even other laboratories. The person who held the new position would need technical laboratory expertise and extensive Internet skills. Jerry was the man for the job. Believing that the Internet held great promise for the future, Jerry had signed on early, before the Net was flooded with hackers and neophytes. He learned his way around and became familiar with search engines and communication techniques. He even learned how to create Web pages. Before he went in for his interview, he searched the Net for information about his prospective employer. He learned about the company's products, safety record, financial history, and goals for the future. And during the interview, he offered some ideas for improving the company's online presentation. Understandably, the manager who interviewed Jerry was impressed with his preparation. And three weeks later, Jerry started his new job. He'd proven his Internet skills, and he'd shown a willingness to take initiative. His first assignment was to implement the good ideas he raised during his interview.

Six months after Jerry left to take his new position, his old company went under. All the employees found themselves jobless and scrambling to find new positions. But by then, Jerry had already settled in, acclimated to his new employer, and no longer needed his anxiety medication. By taking responsibility for himself and his situation, Jerry did more than help himself find a new job. He also helped himself feel better and get better in a more stable environment. By meeting his challenge—and his anxiety—with courage and responsibility, Jerry increased his feelings of self-esteem and gained confidence in his ability to handle a tough situation.

Strength and Weakness

No one knows better than an employer that each person brings a different set of strengths and weaknesses to a job—not just professional skills, but personal qualities as well. Some people are quick to anger, easily flustered, poor communicators, reluctant workers. Other people come to a job with a strong set of people skills, solid self-esteem, enthusiasm, humor, drive, and integrity. Each person is different. Each one brings a different lifetime of struggle, enlightenment, and preparation. Jerry brought a lifetime of mild depression and anxiety, mixed with a strong work ethic, a powerful intellect, and determination to overcome the emotions that dragged him down. By the choices he made and the actions he took, Jerry helped himself do just that. And while Jerry faced more defined mental health obstacles than most of us do, the point remains the same. In this day and age, you need to be more diligent than ever to set standards and make choices that will help you survive with your self-esteem and your professional future intact. You need to take personal responsibility. No one else can or will do it for you. It's up to you to prepare as best you can for the present and the future. You need to make the most of yourself.

That seems hard to do at a time when we feel out of control, scared, and anxious about work. But no time feels like the perfect time. Hard as it may seem, the best thing you can do is to just start, and start right now. Wherever you are in your life and your emotional journey, do what you can. The first step is to assess where you are. Think about the standards you set for yourself, the code of behavior by which you judge yourself. Is it realistic? Is it fair? Is it honorable? Is it tough enough, or maybe too tough? Pretend you've become your boss and try to look at your work and your attitude objectively, as though you were another person. Then pretend you've become a coworker and try to look at who you are to that person. Forget about the excuses and rationalizations for why you behave the way you do. If you look as objectively as possible, you may see qualities you can change about yourself, characteristics you can focus and refine. By setting realistic standards for yourself, you can increase your chance of surviving a company layoff emotionally and professionally intact—whether you lose your job or keep it.

Appropriate Responsibility

It's tempting in these days of job insecurity to set your standards as low as you can get away with—to exert the minimum effort, to resist becoming invested in your company, to complain and drag your feet, and to shirk responsibility for any new project that comes your way. After all, your company could fire you at any minute, no matter how much seniority you have. Why give your best effort every day if you'll just be fired in return? This reaction is understandable. But at some point, it's going to backfire on you. It's becoming very clear, in our corporate environment, that performing to the minimal level of expectation no longer makes the cut. If you look at your performance and your attitude objectively, and you find that this description fits, you run the risk of losing your job for a good reason. When company executives are looking to downsize, they *will* remove the dead wood first. Do you blame them? If you don't care enough about your own reputation to work hard and smart, why should they keep you as part of the progressive team they're trying to build?

In contrast to this picture, I've found that many people set their standards impossibly high. This unrealistic expectation can come out in many unique ways, all related in some measure to self-esteem. One example is the perfectionist. This is the person who must be better than good to be acceptable to self. Often, this person feels second best and has to try harder than everyone else to make up for it. But usually, the rewards of trying for perfection feel good only for a moment. Then, like a drug for an addict, the good feelings fade away, leaving the person with emptiness once again. If this description rings true for you, put yourself in the shoes of your boss and coworkers. Ask yourself honestly whether your unrealistic standards for yourself could be driving other people away. Do other people find you difficult to approach? Do they think you're a snob? Are you unable to relax? Are you unyielding and inflexible? Are you anxious about the smallest (sometimes imagined) problems? If so, understand that, in your quest for perfection, you may be setting yourself apart, behind an emotional wall where your colleagues can't reach you, can't befriend you, can't become part of the net that might save you if you start to fall. In the long run, this kind of emotional isolation and wasted obsessive thinking will hurt you and your career. Also remember that many employers would love to have a staff of perfectionists just like you— people who will give their all to the job, people who will continue working until they reach the perfection they crave. But while working this way might actually help your career (as long as you don't waste time bogged down in details), don't overlook the negative effect it will probably exert on the rest of your life.

Then there's the person with a chip on each shoulder, who lives in fear of making a mistake, never wants to take a risk, never wants to be exposed as the failure he feels he is. This person is devastated by criticism or correction, and may receive it with considerable defensiveness, even a touch of paranoia. Unfortunately, if your low self-esteem causes you to react in the way I've just described, it may place you high on the list if your company decides to downsize. Why? Because, frankly, your superiors can judge you only by your behaviors and your performance. If you're timid and unwilling to take a risk, or if you're brash and defensive to cover your insecurity, you won't be as stellar a performer as many businesses demand these days.

Finally, there's the angry, arrogant person who rides roughshod over everyone nearby, belittling and humiliating other people in an attempt to feel better about self. This person seems to enjoy pointing out other people's mistakes, takes credit for their good ideas, and self-aggrandizes at any opportunity. A person who acts like this wants to feel stronger and smarter by picking on the mistakes and weaknesses of other people. If you have a streak of this kind of behavior, beware. Even more than the other manifestations of low self-esteem, this one is bound to backfire. After all, it's tough to stand by a person who tends to be cruel. And if you're a supervisor, you don't have a prayer of a chance of creating the kind of staff you need: focused, motivated people who feel valued and supported at work.

Inappropriate anger and low self-esteem are just two examples of the kind of personal qualities that can damage your chance of professional success. They're common problems in our culture and they appear in many guises. But as I said before, every person is different. The qualities you'll need to work on are as unique as you are. The key for all of us—those who set impossibly high standards, those who set unacceptably low standards, and everyone in between—is to learn to take an *appropriate* level of personal responsibility for our behaviors. We must assess ourselves objectively and develop the confidence, self-respect, and empathy we need to interact well with other people and work with pride, integrity, and initiative. Maybe you need to work on your social skills. Maybe you need to improve your appearance and your vocabulary. Maybe you're lagging behind in technical skills. Whoever you are, whichever characteristics define you, you can benefit from taking a hard-nosed, objective look at yourself and how you function at work. If you've been laid off, consider whether your personality and work habits had anything to do with it. If they did, work on cultivating the traits you need to become attractive to prospective employers. (If you *always* blame yourself or you *always* blame others, consider psychotherapy as a way to build a more balanced view of causes and effects.) If you haven't been laid off yet, start now. Make yourself into the marketable person you want to be, step by step, right where you are.

Staying Intact

Issues of personality and performance are complex and, in some cases, may take years to untangle. In the meantime, if you lose your job, you need to keep your mental and physical health intact to get yourself through this tough period and the personal changes it may

Secrets of the Job Search

In the past 16 years, thousands of unemployed people have sought help from the nationally known outplacement firm Challenger, Gray & Christmas. If you hired this seasoned firm to help you find a job, what would its experts tell you? Among other things, says executive vice president John Challenger, they'd tell you that employers these days are looking for "adaptable, flexible people who can fit right in— people who can get along with others, people who have current expertise in the company's area of need, people who won't have a lengthy learning curve."

If you fit that mold, says Challenger, finding a good job may not be all that tough. In fact, the average length of time his clients spend searching for a job is "the lowest we've seen it in 16 years of tracking. As of third quarter 1996, the median job search lasted 3.3 months.

"It's surprising news to some people that we have a very strong hiring economy right now," he says. "But with all the downsizing happening at the same time, the overall picture is quite turbulent. Companies are looking for good people and are quick to hire. But they're also quick to let go."

The best way to find your next good job, says Challenger, is to "stay state-of-the-art in your field and be able to point out significant accomplishments in the past three to five years. You need long experience in your field too, but what you've done in the recent past is what makes you very hireable."

Also, if you lose your job at 45 or 50 or older, make a commitment to yourself that you won't apologize or be defensive about your age. "Most middle-aged people assume that no company will want to hire them because they're too old," Challenger explains. "This is absolutely not true. Companies need experience they can put to use now, not six months from now when someone who knows the theory finally gets over the learning curve. So stop being apologetic. There's no reason to be."

Finally, urges Challenger, "you've got to get out and see people. It's difficult even for the most self-assured CEO to admit being out of work. Almost everyone wants to search for a job anonymously. But you can't do a search on paper. The more people who know you're out of work, the more people you talk with and look in the eye, the sooner you'll find a job and the better the job you'll get."

If you're well prepared and willing to embark on a dedicated personal search, your odds of finding the job you want are excellent. Adds Challenger, "There are lots and lots of jobs out there. In no way should you assume that you won't get an equivalent or better job than what you had."

require. In fact, maintaining your mental and physical health is the most important thing you can do for yourself, especially in a period of crisis. After all, these are your main personal assets. They'll influence—perhaps define—the course of the rest of your working life.

Good mental health has a great deal to do with feeling that you have a purpose, that you're *doing* something. But as we've seen in earlier chapters, loss of a job commonly causes people to feel that they've lost their purpose. So what should you do if you lose your job and your sense of purposefulness goes too? The best thing to do, espe-

cially at first, is to recreate it. Make a schedule for yourself. Get up in
the morning, take a shower, and get dressed. If it's hard to motivate
yourself to follow through on this plan, then make appointments in
the morning so you have no choice. Make it so you have something
every day for which you're required to get up and get going. If you
don't have a job interview, do something else that will help you get
your next job. If you don't have great computer skills, take this time
to get them. If you don't know how to get around on the Internet,
now's your chance. Use this opportunity to renew contacts with colleagues. Have lunch with friends. Volunteer your skills at a local charity or community organization and learn something new while you
help someone out. Most of all, don't apologize for being out of work.
And don't hide it. The more people who know you're out of work,
the sooner you'll be back at work.

In addition to creating a daily routine for yourself, make a point
of getting regular physical exercise. Also, if you've ever found comfort in the spiritual or religious dimension of life, pursue it again.
See if it still has meaning for you. If you feel relaxed and peaceful in
the company of pets, spend more time with them. These pursuits
will help you restore the sense of meaning and contribution that
work lends to most people's lives. If you suddenly have a void in
your life where you used to have work, you may feel that you're in
a vacuum and on the verge of flying apart. Activities like these will
help you shift your energy to something positive. You can learn and
give and interact. Keep in mind that work is community. Work is a
place for social interaction. Work is a place for defining your contribution to society. It's not just a way of earning a living. It's a way
of life. You have to find ways of replacing all those functions if
you're not working.

The net effect of maintaining your schedule and your sense of
purpose will be an increased feeling of control. You'll feel that you're
doing something. You'll know that you're making progress. The alternative will probably be to sit at home watching television in your
sweats, waiting for an unemployment check or a miraculous phone

call. But this kind of isolation and inactivity only leads to negative thinking and raises your risk of clinical depression. Typically, it's not helpful at all. The best thing to do when you lose your job is to re-establish the purpose and routine you used to have there.

A Can-Do Attitude

The biggest secret to maintaining your sense of purpose and routine is in your attitude. You'll hear a great deal about attitude in chapter 13. For now, however, I want to say that gaining control over your attitude is an important part of getting back that general sense of control after losing a job. As you saw in chapters 1 and 2, there are plenty of things we can't control. We might as well give up trying. But there are some other things we can and should try to control. Attitude is one of them.

I truly believe that, as long as you're thinking positively and constructively, there's no end to what you can do. It may not be easy. You may find yourself in a worst-case scenario. But there's always a best way to get through it. A can-do attitude can help you find the way. In fact, attitude alone can take you to many heights in life that you otherwise would not have reached. I know people still embarking on major life changes at 70 and 80 years old. They're able to do it because they're convinced they can. If one route doesn't work, they'll find an alternative. The key is to try to use everything in your environment to your advantage to help you act in a way and obtain results that you think will be in your favor. It takes energy and initiative, of course. It takes willingness and courage and optimism to request interviews, take courses, talk with people about the economy or job opportunities, look into self-employment or other business solutions, devise creative ways to survive and thrive in an altered world. You should—and you can—take charge of your attitude and use it to your advantage.

By the way, let me say something about that word *should*. There was a fad going around the pop psychology world a while back that told us to stop using the word should. It suggested that we spend too much time worrying over what we *should* be doing and being and not enough time giving ourselves the freedom to do and be what we really want. I understand the positive motivation behind this fad, but I don't think it's wise to adopt a life philosophy that leaves out the word *should*. There are some things we *should* be and *should* do. We just need to pick them carefully. For example, I should show a good role model to my children and the people around me. I should be able to cope with the unpredictable events life hands me and, after an appropriate period of emotion or mourning, come out the other side relatively intact. After all, sooner or later, everyone has to deal with something difficult. No one gets off scot-free. It's a matter of setting up reasonable expectations for yourself.

So it's not a matter of keeping *shoulds* out of your life. It's a matter of choosing reasonable ones. If you're in the Great Depression, for example, and you think you should be able to earn $50,000 a year, you're going to have to alter that *should* because it doesn't mesh with reality. Likewise, when you're in the middle of this downsizing trend and you think you should have been able to keep your job no matter what, you're going to have to alter that *should* because it doesn't mesh with reality either. Choose your *shoulds* carefully, so they're realistic and provide you with support instead of tearing at your self-esteem. You have to get your frame of reference, and then modify it based on the conditions of society at the time.

For example, instead of telling yourself you should have been able to keep your job, try this. You should be proud of the way you and your family are coping with it. You should be convinced that you can get through anything better if you get through it together. When you talk to your children, tell them that you're the kind of family who can get through this and be okay. We're all going to work together and we're going to figure this out. These are hard times for us and hard times for America. We're going to do the best we can, learn as much as we can, work together as much as we can, and help other people as much as we can. That's what you should take pride in—helping people in similar situations, getting back to the really important values, trying to figure out what really counts, and forgiving yourself. You can't be responsible for major economic shifts in the world. That's not your fault. That's not your shame.

This process of carefully choosing your *shoulds* is analogous to the standards we talked about earlier. Are the standards you set for yourself reasonable? Are they consonant with economic and personal reality? As you really think about it, you'll find that the place you put your expectations is the place you'll find—or lose—your satisfaction.

1 0

What Did You Expect?

THE DAY DAWNED bright and crisp on little Timmy's 10th birthday. As soon as his eyes opened, the towheaded youngster bounded out of bed and scampered down the stairs toward the living room, the room where he knew his gifts would be waiting. He sprinted down the hall, skidded around the corner, and there they were. One from Mom and Dad, and one from Gram and Gramps, each brightly wrapped and topped with a shiny bow. He tore into the carefully creased paper on the first box and barely stopped to look at the muscled action figures packed inside. Instead, he dropped them quickly, grabbed up the other box, skimmed off the wrapping paper, pried open the lid, and pawed excitedly into the tissue. Then his face fell.

Standing in the doorway, Timmy's mother watched him throw the snap-together model onto the carpet and plunge his face into his upturned hands. As soon as she approached him, Timmy's face contorted and he began to cry, sobbing and gulping that he didn't get what he wanted. No amount of hugging and explaining would console him, because Tim had fully expected to find the toy he wanted most. Even though he loved action figures. Even though the model was his favorite war plane. They weren't good enough. He had expected something else. And because his expectations were so strong, they ruined his ability to enjoy the good things he received.

It's not just children who have expectations. We all have them. We live by them. They help us excel. They help us set goals. Unmet, they can leave us battling disappointment, anger, and resentment. How you react to the various situations that arise in your life—good and bad, major and minor, easy and hard—depends largely on what you expect from yourself and your world.

Typically, expectations arise from a blend of observations, desires, and hopes. Rarely do we even analyze or question our expectations. We expect, for example, that children will outlive their parents. We have the luxury of that expectation, because children typically *do* outlive their parents in our society. So we can observe it to be usually true, we want it to be true, we hope it will be true. In fact, this is such a deep-seated and profound expectation that, when a child dies, the grieving process is much longer and more arduous than when an older loved one dies. It is perhaps the most painful single event for a person to face. We can all understand why. Of course it's painful to lose a parent. But in general, when a parent dies in old age, you can find a way to accept it. You may even feel fortunate that you had so much time together. Your aged parent lived a long and fruitful life, had opportunities and experiences, bore children and raised them to adulthood. For this person, passing on is well within the expected, natural order of things. The death of a child is not. We have different expectations for our children. Likewise, you expect that you and your spouse will have a long life together. But what if he dies of a heart attack at 43? What if she dies of cancer at 45? Your deep-seated expectation is unmet, making this inherently difficult event that much harder to cope with.

Naturally, expectations about work wield a major influence on your levels of satisfaction and stress in that area of your life. Each person brings an individual set of expectations to work based on childhood dreams, personal wishes, family background, education level, financial status, and many other factors. But in America, we also tend to have some collective expectations about work—expectations that may no longer be realistic, expectations that may be setting us up for devastation in this time of downsizing and turbulence.

A Steady Course

One of our most deeply held expectations about work is that we will progress on a relatively steady course. We'll get promotions. We'll get raises. By working to a reasonable level of competence, over time, we'll be "successful." In general, this means that we'll engage in a series of what we consider to be age-appropriate stages. I mentioned them earlier. In our 20s, we expect to choose a career and get started in it. In our 30s, we expect to gain experience and status. In our 40s, we expect to have enviable expertise and considerable earning power. In our 50s and 60s, we begin to rearrange priorities. We think about helping, mentoring. And we expect to start thinking about retirement. These stages and age ranges aren't absolute. But in general, we expect to progress through our working lives. In today's economy, for a massive number of people, this expectation is being shattered.

For much of the past 50 years, Americans have been taught that if we work hard, we'll be rewarded. So here you are. You've worked 16 years in the accounting department. Your corporation gets bought by a bigger corporation. The bigger corporation has its own accounting department, and you get fired. You get a pink slip. You get downsized, rightsized, reorganized. Doesn't matter what you call it. The effect is the same. You're out of a job. Here you've "given 16 years of your life" to the corporation. Maybe your marriage has suffered because you worked too hard. Maybe your kids are angry because you didn't seem available enough. And everything that you worked for and sacrificed yourself (and your family) for is gone in a flash. You're left saying, "Wait. This isn't right. I held up my end of the bargain. But my employer didn't hold up its end. I've been betrayed."

No. You haven't been betrayed. You had an expectation that was understandable at the time you started work, but unrealistic in today's business climate. The expectations we've developed about our economy and our workplaces feel as if they're the natural order of things, like children outliving their parents. But they're not the same. Everything in the business world is changing. Businesses and the people who work for them are subject to enormous forces in the world economy just now. You can't control them. Neither can the company you work for. As a result, we need to begin a period of defining and rethinking all of our expectations about work. We need to put things in a more realistic historical perspective. We need to expect changes and turbulence in the workplace, be ready for them, and respond accordingly.

That doesn't mean you won't or shouldn't have strong emotions about losing your job. After all, it's one thing to decide to quit. It's quite another to have your job taken from you, against your will, by some external force. Understandably, it's hard to maintain your self-esteem under these circumstances. It's hard to avoid placing blame. It's hard not to feel ashamed. But after you cry, after you grieve, after you realize that your expectations were misplaced, you learn from it and you go on. This resilience is the real key to success.

Let me say something here about shame. In general, a feeling of shame arises when you don't meet your expectations of yourself. Throughout life and especially during childhood, we each form a set of expectations for ourselves. We form these expectations out of what we hear from our parents, from our neighbors and friends, from teachers, from the media, and from our own feelings. We interpret all this information and intuition into a picture of our ideal self—a personalized set of expectations. Everyone has a different set of personal expectations. A family like the Kennedys will probably have different expectations of themselves than the typical American family. A family of artists may have modest financial expectations, but great personal pressures to be creative. A family of successful entrepreneurs may have above-average financial expectations of themselves and their children. Based on who they are, what they have, what they want, and where they've come from, people expect different things from themselves.

Let's say you picture yourself as a manager at the local bank, you belong to the country club, you live in a spacious four-bedroom house you bought for your family, and you send your children to the local private elementary school. If you lose your job, your expectations and your actual situation now differ. There's some level of dissonance between how you believe you deserve to live and what your employer seems to be telling you you're worth by handing you a pink slip. Plus, without a job, you may not have the financial power to surround yourself with the things that reflect and support your picture of yourself. If your self-esteem is shaky anyway, you may not have a strong sense of who you are without those external reminders. So you begin to fear that you're not good enough to live up to your expectations. That it's due to some defect in you. And you feel shame. But please understand that this feeling is not because you did something wrong and not because you aren't good enough. It's because of that dissonance between your expectations and your actual situation at this moment. Let me remind you that you are the same person you were before the layoff. At this time in our economic history, your layoff probably has nothing to do with your competence or who you are as a person.

No Fair!

Another expectation that we carry close to our hearts and into our workplaces is that life should be fair. When asked straight out, many would deny thinking that life is fair. But most of us believe, underneath it all, that we should get what we deserve. What goes around comes around. The problem arises when you narrow that expectation down to the scope of individual events. Then you're begging for trouble.

We all want life to make sense. It's human nature. So we're taught as little children that, if you do the right thing, good things will happen to you as a result. This may be an effective way to civilize people, and it's a simple enough model for children to understand and obey. But as we grow into adults, we have to realize that the world works at a higher level than we can understand—either in its randomness or in its reflection of a God much more complex than we can grasp. Whichever reason is correct, the fact is that life does not necessarily make sense to us. No one promised that everything would tally up equally at the end.

So what can you do with your expectation that life should be fair? What can you do with the unfairness of losing a job? You can grieve. Get angry. Whine. Cry. But in the end, to maintain your mental health, you have to eventually say, "Okay. Life is not fair. Now what can I do to move on in that knowledge?" This may not be an immediate transition. It may take you some time to accept that what happens in life may not make sense. It may not seem fair. But eventually, within a reasonable period of time, you need to decide to move on. Find a way to look at life more optimistically, with acceptance. What's your alternative, after all? The resilient person, the person best able to handle life's curveballs, eventually thinks of these unforeseen and unfair situations as potential avenues to growth. The more you can think this way, the more you'll be able to live it.

To help you swallow the bitter pill of unfairness a little more easily, let's look at just how unfair life is. Oh yes, life is unfair. And for the typical American, life is unfairly blessed. We have it better than a large percentage of the rest of the world just by being born here. Was it fair that you were born here and other people were born in the slums of a Third World country? Is it fair that most Americans live in single-family apartments or spacious houses? You could have been born in a place where you live in a doorway and passersby step over your lifeless body when you die. Yes. It's unfair that you were born here and that you have opportunities unknown to many of the world's citizens. Here in America, nearly everyone experiences profound unfairness from the positive side of the picture. Rather than balking at what we perceive to be life's unfairness, perhaps the better course is one of acknowledging and being grateful for the blessings we have.

The good news about accepting the potential unfairness of life is that it helps you to embrace change as a condition of existence rather than an enemy to be feared and fought. Loss of your job may (and should) lead you to reexamine and reevaluate yourself, your work, your finances, your choices, your expectations. This is a valuable process and one that may lead to increased happiness and satisfaction with yourself and your life. We all tend toward inertia. And most of us make the daily trek to work without much analysis of its benefits and drawbacks in our lives. Losing your job has the potential to alter your expectations about life in a very positive way, if you let it (or a very negative way, if you let it). Remember that every time you're forced to take on a challenge, and you meet it, you get a tremendous sense of empowerment, confidence, peacefulness, and self-esteem. Coping with a layoff may be your biggest challenge yet.

Time or Money

Perhaps the most inherently American of the expectations we harbor about work is that more money (and more things) result in a better life. We even make the assumption that people who bring home more money are worth more *as human beings* than people who bring home less money. But it's important to recognize that a person's value does not fluctuate like a stock on the market. You don't look in the *Wall Street Journal* to see what you're worth today. Of course not, I can hear you saying. That's ridiculous. But now let me take you one step further. Put yourself in these shoes: If I get a raise, I feel like I'm worth more. If I don't get a raise, I feel like I'm worth less. If I drive a new Lexus, I'll feel better than if I drive a used Dodge. Coming closer to home? These are all different ways to express the same idea.

We all think this way to some degree. And I've found that most people question their assumptions and expectations rarely, if at all, especially if those assumptions were adopted early in life. Although there's an almost infinite variation between people and the conclusions we reach as children, it's common to have a thread of childhood assumptions running through your adult thoughts. Money is a subject about which most children develop assumptions. Some children grow up to be people who assume that they need lots of money to be happy. Others assume that having lots of money is our right as Americans. Still others assume that only people who have money can get respect and courtesy. But especially at this time in our history, placing an inordinate emphasis on money, those who have it, and those who don't, will probably bring you only bitterness and resentment.

As I said in earlier chapters, it's only been since World War II that we've even conceived of the concept of job security. In the boom years after the war, businesses needed workers badly. Labor unions flourished. It didn't take long before we believed that a single-family home, a pair of cars, a raise every year, and a prosperous retirement were a guaranteed part of American life. But now, when we worry about that picture fading, when we feel as if we're working harder than ever to stay in the same place, we have to look carefully at the effects our expectations have on our lives, and how we choose to juggle those effects.

In my observation, what many people do to hang onto an overblown financial expectation is to trade their time for the prospect of continued money. Work longer hours. Take work home. Wear a pager 24 hours a day. Carry a mobile phone. Set up a home office. Buy a fax machine for the car. If this description sounds like you, think very carefully about the ramifications of your choices. Analyze closely the effect of trading your time—nearly all of your time, perhaps—to maintain a lifestyle that meets your unquestioned financial expectation. Maybe it's time to question that expectation. If you're currently out of a job, maybe this is the ideal time to question that expectation. Start with questions like these: How much of yourself do you want to sell? How much of your self-image is based on the *things* you have? How much are you substituting things for the relationships and life meaning that we no longer emphasize in this country? How much of your time are you trading away for something less valuable than time? It all comes down to this. Time is all we really have. It's our most valuable asset. We can choose to spend time in an almost infinite number of ways. Some of those ways add real value to our lives. Some of them add only the illusion of value.

Look at it this way. In America, we now have a large population of people willing to work 60-hour, 70-hour, 80-hour weeks. Take a look at this with your eyes wide open and you'll see that unscrupulous employers can make hay with this. The more each person is willing to give, the fewer people the company has to hire. If you're willing to work 80 hours in one week, you're doing the work of two people. This is especially handy if you're on salary. If executives can convince a salaried person to work more hours for the same money, it makes the bottom line look better. So if the bottom line is driving the train, it's in the employer's best interest to squeak every last drop out of every last person. This may be short-sighted, because an exhausted workforce can't possibly maintain production and quality. But it does make for a pretty financial picture, at least temporarily.

Losing Perspective

Why are so many of us willing to put up with this exhausting workload? Because we're scared that our post–World War II expectations may not come to fruition. And because we're losing our perspective on what's really important in life. Many people who give too much to the job do so because they're afraid of being unemployed. If the boss tells you to work 80-hour weeks, you figure you have to or you might find yourself on the street with nothing. It feels as though you have no alternatives. Uncaring employers may subtly encourage this fear. Once again, this tactic may be short-sighted. But at least temporarily, it boosts that bottom line.

The problem with this way of thinking is that it ignores the fact that you always have alternatives, especially in this nation. You are not trapped, and you are not a prisoner. The problem is that many of us are scared to think about alternatives. In general, people are most comfortable with the familiar, even if the familiar borders on miserable. Sometimes, psychologically, we prefer comfortable illusions to the truth. So we trade our time and energy for the illusion of security with an employer. Don't forget that this security is, in fact, an illusion, no matter how many hours (or years) you work. That's what this time in our history is all about.

The other problem is that many workers, especially managers and executives, have become vocal opponents but willing participants in a corporate culture that rewards competitiveness at all costs. These employees derive some degree of superiority from working harder and longer than their colleagues, as though giving their all for the bottom line somehow makes them better or more valuable people overall. I hope, if this describes you, that seeing it spelled out will help you see how misguided a belief it is, even if it does solicit praise from your employer.

Whether you're too scared to cut back to a regular work week or too embroiled in competition to go home, the root issue may be the same. I've found that people tend not to reflect on what they're doing. We don't question our assumptions or analyze our expectations. Frankly, that's one of the benefits of being in therapy. It forces you to look at yourself instead of traveling on automatic pilot. But you don't have to be in therapy to think about who you are, what you're doing, and what you want from your job and from your life. If you've been laid off, now is an excellent time to start. It's important to redefine on a regular basis what you expect from a job in light of the economy, where you are in your personal journey, what you want from your significant relationships, and what you hold as values in your life. Examine whether your expectations are realistic and healthy, and what you expect to have to do to keep a job. As you saw in chapter 4, only you can set these limits for yourself. Only you will know when your work has crossed a boundary that impinges on other important aspects of your life.

Look at the amount of time you devote (or devoted, if you're unemployed) to work. Look at it honestly. Don't shave it or give excuses for it. Just look at it. If you're like most people these days, you're willing to give more to your work than to your family—maybe a lot more. Maybe you're letting your work monopolize you, just so you can maintain that expectation of success. Maybe you tell yourself you're working so hard *for* your family, even though your family might rather have more time with you. Is your job giving you enough to make it worth all this? Pay close attention to that question. Is your work *giving* you enough to make it worth the time and effort you're willing to invest in trying to fulfill your expectation? Many of you are probably thinking that, these days, work doesn't give you much besides a paycheck that seems too small for the amount of labor that went into it. If that's the case, you might want to start making plans to rethink your expectations of success. If you're unemployed, you might want to make plans to avoid getting into this situation again. If you're working and want to keep your job, you might want to think about drawing a line for yourself in the sand. The trick about the line in the sand, however, is that you have to react when the line gets crossed. Otherwise you don't feel good about yourself.

Drawing that line and sticking by it gives you a sense of empowerment. If you decide that you'll work 80 hours a week for one or two weeks, but not as a way of life, you've given yourself some power. If you decide you'll travel two weeks a year but no more, that gives you power. Your employer may still be making decisions for you, but you have the ultimate veto power. What your employer holds is the power to fire you. But if you've set your limits and you get fired for not crossing them, you didn't want that job anyway.

Almighty Dollar

The key to traversing this process of reflection in a healthy way goes back to your expectations about time, money, and the things you can buy with it. It's become a way of life for many Americans to trade time and energy for money at any personal cost. Too many of us then throw that money away on things—pretty things displayed temptingly in television and magazine ads—an unending variety of things we want not because we need them but because they exist. To make matters even worse, most of us go into debt to get these things. And then we're more tightly tied to a job—and more afraid of losing it—

than ever. My intention here is not to minimize the plight of the many Americans struggling to make ends meet, those who truly don't have enough money to purchase what they need. My intention is to sound a wake-up call to the many more who spend too much for what they don't need and sometimes don't even want.

This cycle is a reflection of our expectation that more money and more things will make for a better life. But it doesn't sound like a better life, does it? It sounds more like voluntary enslavement.

America has not always been such a consumption-oriented society. Businesses in this country, through advertising, have created this consumer society in less than 50 years. Now we have a society where one of our chief nonworking activities is shopping. We've been encouraged to spend-spend-spend and borrow-borrow-borrow. We even use the word consumer to describe ourselves. The more you work, the more money you spend; the more money you spend, the more you have to work. This vicious cycle is what keeps businesses going. It's the down side of capitalism, and it's fueled by advertising. I wouldn't wish to live under any other economic system, of course, but it is useful to recognize the pitfalls of our capitalistic culture; it creates a desire among the citizens for things we don't need and provides a means of obtaining even the things we can't afford.

Too many of us have succumbed to the temptation of *things*. We have ever larger homes, more appliances, newer cars, and constant debt. Maybe it's time to rethink the expectation that more money makes a better life and the assumption that your worth is equal to the number of exclusive things that surround you. Especially in a time of job insecurity, this expectation may not serve you from a mental health perspective, from a relationship perspective, or from an employment perspective. We need to rethink our value systems and reach renewed conclusions about what's really important. Then we can reevaluate our relationships with work, money, and time in light of that renewed value system.

Redefined Expectations

The solution is to forgive ourselves, take charge of our lives once again, live within our means, and adopt the philosophy that we work for ourselves. Why do we need to forgive ourselves? Because when people get laid off, the first thing they usually do is berate themselves for neglecting to save money. Don't do that. Don't blame yourself if you don't have a big nest egg, because our society has encouraged us to spend everything we make. Don't hate yourself if you're fired unexpectedly and you don't have a huge savings account. But do use this as an opportunity to decide to live differently. Because in my observation, people who have an abundance of things don't seem to be happier because of it. You need certain things, like food, shelter, and clothing, to meet your basic needs. But once those basic needs are met, your priorities should shift to friendship, family, finding a sense of meaning in life, being involved in a community, creating, giving, teaching your children important lessons for the future—pursuits that really do make a better life. On their deathbeds, people don't usually wish they'd spent more time at work, making more money to buy more stuff.

To begin the process of redefining your expectations about what makes a successful life, start by reevaluating yourself, your work, your finances, and your choices. It's your life. It's your responsibility to take charge of it. There's no better way to take charge financially than by making a budget. For many people, anxiety about money comes from not knowing how much is coming in and how much is going out. Making a budget will fix that problem. Do you know how much you need to pay your fixed bills each month? Do you know whether you're paying out, over time, more than you bring in? You'd be surprised at how many people live constantly in the red and don't really face it until the bills are monstrous. Others simply live in anxiety, too afraid to find out what their financial picture really looks like. All this anxiety exacts a high price, both mentally and physically. Making a budget will help free you from that anxiety; after all, maybe you're worried over nothing.

When you make a budget, the key is to consider more than just money. Don't write down all the things you want and then wrack your brain trying to figure out how to get the money to pay for them. That's backwards. Consider the possibility that working at a job you hate, and constant worry about maintaining your lifestyle, may actually be harder on you than cutting back a bit. In your budget, consider the value of your time, the priorities in your life, the expectations you have for yourself. Then work with all those concepts in finalizing a reasonable financial expectation. Start by paring your budget down to its essential elements. Are you bringing in enough to pay for them, and saving some as well? If so, you can begin to add the nonessential elements while keeping the whole picture within your comfort zone—and within your means. Don't bother to add the things intended just to impress your neighbors or your ego. Set a reasonable number on what you think is "enough" and then create a satisfying life out of it.

If you're laid off, your budget may need to change. After all, if a boat springs a leak, you don't stubbornly cling to everything in the boat and force it to sink. You throw some of it overboard. Maybe it's time for some of us to think about what we can throw overboard for now. Maybe we should do a little downsizing ourselves. When we get through this time in our economy, maybe we'll get back the stuff that we threw overboard. Or maybe by then we'll realize we don't want it back. Maybe by then we'll realize that the truly valuable things in life are peace of mind, family, friendships, enjoyment—not just things.

Above all, whether you're working or not, remember what money can and can't buy for you. Specifically, money can't buy back time. That's why so many people have a midlife crisis. Too many young people squander time on the promise of money, only to realize—at 45 or 50 or 55—that time is all we have. So they try to become young again. They get divorces from their middle-aged spouses. They date people young enough to be their children. They try desperately, futilely, to get that time back. It's common to experience midlife crisis and there's nothing particularly bad about it as long as you don't destroy your life over it. But wouldn't it be better, and easier, to redefine your expectations and priorities earlier, before you get into such a predicament? Wouldn't you rather be rich in friends, loved ones, physical and mental health, traditions, spiritual satisfaction, learning, creating, *living* instead of rich in debt and dedicated to spending money?

There's an interesting dividend to reducing your dependence on things. Life seems to slow down. Suddenly, you feel as if you have more time. And you probably do. In some ways, the things you surround yourself with can be oppressive. You have to support them, maintain them, think about them, make decisions about them, worry about damaging them, keep them organized and tidy. They require something from you. They take some of your mental energy. And when it comes to analyzing and redefining your expectations for your life and your work, you need all the mental energy you can muster.

Real Satisfaction

Once you decide to alter your assumption about the importance of money in your life, you're well on your way to creating realistic expectations and a more contented, less anxious future. Getting laid off may actually assist this process. Certainly, it can be a difficult and painful experience. But it may also force you to start the reevaluation that leads to real satisfaction. One of the benefits of being under stress is that you have the opportunity to let that stress push you toward deciding what's really important and what isn't.

I think we'd all agree that having enough money to get by is really important. Just don't forget that "enough" is a relative concept. A person who has four cars, a plane, and two yachts may feel that two cars and one yacht simply isn't enough. But a person who doesn't have even one car would feel blessed beyond imagining. So when you decide what, for you, is enough, try to keep the bigger picture in mind in addition to weighing the characteristics specific to your own life.

Depending on your wage and your employment status, you may

have to rework your definition of "enough" from time to time, possibly to a lower level than you had hoped. But if you spend your time being unhappy about that fact and envious of people who have more than you do, you won't even be able to enjoy what you do have. Did you get that? If you spend your life being envious and ungrateful, you won't receive pleasure from what you do have. So, in essence, your envy can make you think you have nothing when, in fact, you may be surrounded by valuable people, relationships, opportunities, talents, and, yes, things. No matter how much you have, someone else will always have more. So don't spend your time in a way that robs you of your life. And don't forget that time is your most precious commodity. If worrying over things is soaking up your time, then—for the sake of your mental health—start reducing your reliance on them by rethinking your values and changing your ideas about what's important.

I would never suggest that you have to give up everything and become an ascetic to be mentally healthy. The question is one of priorities. What is most important to you? Is it the image you want to project to your neighbors because of the car you drive? Is it the importance you feel when you spend a wad of money in a store? Or is it your spouse, your kids, an evening of conversation with people you genuinely enjoy? If you tend toward an overreliance on things, be warned. They'll never be able to give you what you truly need. The effect is too temporary. Driving your new red Ferrari is great and it impresses everyone. But if you bought it as a status symbol, it will eventually lose its impact, leaving you yearning for yet another, more impressive status symbol.

Ultimately, spending money to get things will not make you happy. In fact, it feels pretty empty. You may feel an initial rush when you buy something, rather like taking a drug. But in this case, it's a very short-acting drug that you'll have to take again and again. I call it consumer therapy. And it doesn't work. I once had a patient who went to an estate sale in Pebble Beach, a very exclusive area in northern California. This patient discovered literally closets and closets full of new, unused merchandise for sale, original price tags still dangling—hundreds of outfits, dozens of leather bags, countless shoes. Obviously, the deceased woman's pleasure in acquiring this vast horde of things lasted only from the store to the closet, because she never got them out again. So you see, there's never enough if your expectations about fulfillment and success are misplaced.

There are plenty of ways to maintain healthy attitudes about the things around you. For example, don't feel bad about using things as a way to tell people about yourself. If you collect fountain pens or books or baseball caps, and you display them in your house, that's not about being important. That's a perfectly acceptable avenue for telling people who you are. Don't feel bad about buying quality either. It's excess—conspicuous consumption—that I'm talking about: buying more things than you can balance in your life simply because you hold the unquestioned expectation that more money and more things make a better life and define you as a better human being. The economic reality that we find ourselves in just now may do us the unexpected favor of forcing us to question, and alter, that expectation.

Maybe, if we're fortunate, we'll come to appreciate ourselves without all the superficial decorations and labels of material things. Maybe our economic reality will also allow us to identify good and healthy expectations, like this one: Expect, if you lead a life in keeping with your ethics, morality, and spirituality, that you'll be able to work and love in an effective manner, that you'll be able to look in the mirror of your mind and like the person you are, and that you'll be able to contribute to the world and to your own sense of well-being. I can't think of a more successful life than that.

The Worth of a Soul

W HEN SOMEONE comes to see me after having lost a job, one of the words I typically hear early in the first conversation is "worthless." I feel worthless. Many people battle feelings of worthlessness and failure when something goes wrong at work. And naturally, most of us still think of a layoff as the ultimate example of a workday gone wrong. But if you think more deeply about it, you'll recognize intuitively that a human being is worth infinitely more than any job can ever bestow—and infinitely more than the loss of that job can take away. In fact, if you listen carefully to your rising feelings of worthlessness, you may come to see that they have nothing at all to do with your layoff.

Such was the case with Susan McGuire. From Susan, we can all learn something about the struggle for feelings of self-worth—and the sweetness of attaining them.

Illusion of Confidence

Perched stiffly on the edge of a comfortable chair in my office, Susan McGuire looked decidedly *un*comfortable. This was her first visit to

a psychiatrist's office, and it seemed obvious that the prospect of re-
vealing herself made Susan want to bolt from the room. But she was
brave and truly wanted to help herself feel better; eventually, Susan
slid her body carefully backward into the deep cushion, took a long
breath, and slowly began to talk to me.

Attractive and immaculately groomed, Susan McGuire had wavy
dark hair trimmed neatly to her shoulders, bright blue eyes, and pale
skin with a sprinkling of tiny freckles across the bridge of her nose.
She wore an expensive silk suit several shades darker than her eyes, a
boldly patterned scarf, and unscuffed high-heeled shoes. To the outside world, she was the picture of a woman confident and comfortable with herself. But the picture was an illusion—and Susan knew it.

In fact, Susan felt herself in a mighty struggle. A struggle between her family, her job, and her view of herself. Over the course
of several visits, Susan talked with me about her feelings of unhappiness, emptiness, and confusion. She had difficulty pinning these feelings on any one part of her life, but she felt somehow responsible for
them. Admitting feelings of failure, even in the privacy of a psychiatrist's office, is difficult and scary. And Susan was scared. She was
scared to tell me—to tell herself—that her life might have been one
long mistake, failing her children and herself in blind pursuit of a
bigger and better job.

At All Costs

All her life, Susan had been driven to succeed. And succeed she did.
Starting as an administrative assistant at a massive high-tech company,
Susan steadily climbed the corporate ladder to higher and higher positions. By the time she came to see me, Susan had worked for the
same company for more than 10 years and had become director of
customer service for all the company's new electronic products. Her
job offered prestige and good money. But it required extraordinarily
long hours, frequent travel to satellite offices, white-knuckle "account-
ability" meetings with the company's president and senior staff, and

total availability in moments of supposed crisis. Susan carried a pager and a cellular phone everywhere she went, even when she came to see me. More than once, she stopped talking in mid–sentence, grabbed for her pager, fished the telephone from her briefcase (which she always carried), and anxiously asked if I minded waiting a moment while she called in.

How had she come to be so tied to her work, I wondered? If feelings of failure perfused her family life, why did she continue to devote herself so singularly to work? Naturally, some of the most important answers lay in her childhood. Susan told me she'd grown up on the east coast, an only child, on a lavish estate surrounded by manicured gardens. Her father was the groundskeeper for the sprawling property and spent his days mowing, pruning, planting, and admiring the beauty of his efforts. Susan and her parents lived in a refurbished carriage house a few hundred yards down a mossy path from the main house, "the mansion," as Susan described it. And although Susan's father seemed peacefully content with his calling in life, her mother was not. Quick to criticize her husband and often defensive with the estate's owners, Susan's mother could barely conceal her bitterness that God had provided so little for her while providing so much for her husband's employers. If only her husband had more ambition, Susan's mother once told her, the family might have "made it."

Lofty Goals

It quickly became clear to me that Susan had grown up literally in the shadow of privilege. But she had little of her own. Her father couldn't even afford tuition at the local community college. And as all children do, this man's daughter had wordlessly, unknowingly taken a portion of her mother's feelings as her own. She felt embarrassed when she described her father as a groundskeeper and shame at his lack of accomplishment. Susan's early lessons created in her a drive for financial success above all else. And when, at 19, she found a man who shared her views, she married him barely a month after his college commencement ceremony. Susan's husband pushed her to have children quickly, start them growing, and join him in their quest for financial bounty. He urged her to find work almost immediately after their third child started kindergarten, teasing that she was "way behind" in the wage-earning department. Her husband's assumption that Susan could never match his salary only drove her harder, she told me. Above all else, she wanted her husband's approval and, somewhere in her child's mind, her mother's approval as well. She tried to get that approval the only way she knew how—through an important job and a fat paycheck.

Over the next 12 years, Susan and her husband met many of their lofty financial goals. But it was frequently at the expense of their home lives. Because they both worked for the same company, they drew more than their share of transfers. In fact, Susan and her family moved five times at the company's bidding. Sometimes they had to move in the middle of the school year, uprooting their children and tearing them from friends and routines so their parents could continue climbing the corporate ladder. And now, at 42, Susan feared that something had gone terribly wrong. She felt distanced from her husband and dismissed by her children. Her oldest son, now 22 and working toward a Wharton MBA, scoffed at her career and considered it scant compensation for requiring him to become an adult at age 12. Her middle boy, a junior at a small liberal arts college, confessed to his younger sister that he dreamed of becoming a forest ranger in the Rockies. But he never told his mother. Susan's 17-year-old daughter had grown obstinate at a young age and slouched aimlessly with a group of teenagers whom Susan didn't know and whose parents never seemed to be home. This was not the life that Susan had envisioned, not the dream her mother had described, and she couldn't figure out what went wrong. But she felt it must be her fault.

A New Assignment

As we began to uncover and work through Susan's feelings about her job, her family, and herself, a curious thing happened. She got transferred to another job. And then another. And then another. All in less than a year. It seemed executives at her bloated company wanted to streamline, to re-engineer, to run a leaner, meaner operation more competitive in their fast-paced field. Customer service—her department—was the first to go. Instead of using in-house staff to solve customer problems, executives predicted that they could save money by contracting out for the service. Two weeks after Susan was notified, her entire department of 83 people got laid off. Shocked and shaken, the only one left, Susan began a temporary position as liaison with the new customer service company. Believing the best, Susan tackled her new job with enthusiasm. She got acquainted with people at the service company, talked with them often, helped bring them up to speed, and offered them steady assistance whenever they needed it. Susan even agreed to spend two weeks a month on-site at their facility, a thousand miles from home. The demands of her job grew larger than ever.

After a few months, Susan's boss thanked her for helping out and announced that he had a new "assignment" for her. In her new job, Susan was to create reports that tracked customer calls, the length of time they waited on hold, how many hung up in frustration, how many complaints were successfully resolved, and how much the company was paying for customer service in relation to the number of calls taken. Early on, Susan told me she didn't enjoy the work. It seemed to be costing the company as much as ever to use the outside service company. But she had no authority to implement improvements and no possibility of reinstating her department. Plus, she had lost the part of her job that brought her the most satisfaction.

Susan thrived on working closely with other employees, solving their problems, and helping systems run smoothly. She thought of herself as a good boss and, as department supervisor, considered each day a challenge and an opportunity. But now, sitting alone in her office with her computer and phone logs, she grew bored and unhappy with her tedious assignment. Eventually, she worked up the nerve to tell her boss how she felt. He told her he wished he could help, but it was a bad time to make waves. At least she still had a job. And they hadn't even cut her salary.

Less than two months later, they did exactly that. Susan came to my office blustering and frustrated. Not only had they cut her salary, she told me, but now she reported to a director—who used to be her peer—instead of to a vice president. And they'd dropped her job two grade levels. Her ego was badly bruised, her morale in decline. Susan said she didn't know why they were treating her so badly, why she wasn't worth more to them.

Four weeks later, she too got laid off. Quivering, she told me that her new boss had come to her tiny office late one afternoon and asked her to attend a quick meeting. Bring your purse and your briefcase along, he'd said grimly. They walked to the personnel department. The director, stiff and formal though she'd known him for years, told her how hard "the company" tried to find a place for her. But now that her department was gone, they felt her position didn't fit the firm's new direction. They gave her a week's severance for every year of work—three months' pay for 12 years' labor. The personnel director handed her a stack of papers to sign. He asked for the security card she used to enter the building. And he escorted her out the front door and onto the sidewalk. Come back Saturday at 10, he said, to finish cleaning out your office.

The effect on Susan was immediate and striking. The power-suited picture of corporate success stopped appearing at my office. Instead, a gaunt and deflated woman took her place, a woman who stopped wearing makeup and jewelry, who barely combed her hair, a woman who within a matter of weeks had descended into a dark well of depression. Before her layoff, Susan wondered why her strenuous efforts in life had left her unfulfilled. Afterward, she wondered why she was alive. Despondent and withdrawn, Susan sunk deeper into despair. I became her only link with the outside world. The one endeavor that fed Susan's sense of self-worth was gone. Now, she told me, her failure was complete. She actually called herself "worthless." The emotional account that held her self-esteem was bankrupt.

Worthless

Susan's story, while unique in its details, includes many elements common to the laid-off people I treat professionally and know personally. Above all, her feelings of self-worth stemmed largely from her ability to gain approval from someone else. Rather than looking to her inner self, Susan looked to other people to validate her worth—her husband, her mother, her employer. She leveraged her self-esteem on the size of her paycheck. Loss of her job, loss of that paycheck, closed the primary door that Susan left open to feeling good about herself.

Although every person's story is different, the underlying rationale always goes something like this when a layoff leads to feelings of worthlessness: *My employer must have considered me worthless or I wouldn't have been laid off. And if my employer thinks I'm worthless, then it must be true.* How wrong this is! This kind of thinking gives your employer far too much power and influence over you. It simply adds insult to the layoff injury. And, lo and behold, you're the one wielding the insult against yourself.

There's no doubt that getting laid off feels terrible. Losing your job is a traumatic event that's bound to raise strong emotions. But by succumbing to feelings of worthlessness, you only succeed in punishing yourself for something completely out of your control. This kind of emotion hurts you more than it heals you. If you're like most people in this situation, the problem is that you've entrusted your feelings of self-worth to an outside force, in this case your employer. That's a mistake. An employer, a salary, another person, or any entity outside yourself is too fickle a place to plant your feelings of worth. And in this era of downsizing and reorganizing, it's a more precarious position than ever.

Consider the Source

If you peel away all the outer layers of hurt, fear, betrayal, and individual circumstances, the fact is that you have feelings of worthlessness not because you lost your job, but because you're looking to the wrong source for your feelings of self-worth. You're looking outside of yourself for something that you can only find within yourself. Never forget that you have an intrinsic self-worth that doesn't change, no matter what happens to you or what other people think or do or say. Self-worth is not something that a spouse, a friend, an employer, or anyone else can give you. You already have it. The real question is whether you believe it. That's where the concept we call "self-esteem" comes in.

While your intrinsic worth never changes no matter what, your self-esteem might, at least temporarily. To be sure, life's many traumas may temporarily damage your opinion of yourself and batter your feelings of self-esteem. These traumas may be connected to experiences and lessons learned way back when you were a very small child. And they can be amplified by current relationships and life events. Whatever their origin, they can create areas of emotional weakness and vulnerability if you let them. But fortunately, it's never too late to learn techniques to battle back against the effect of events that damage your self-esteem.

How can you develop a healthy concept of self-worth? All things being equal, the easiest way is to be born to a mentally healthy mother and father, to inherit the genes for good mental health, and to be just plain lucky in the way life turns out. Obviously, not all of us will have these blessings. But fortunately, even as an adult, you can help to improve your self-esteem and restore your feelings of self-worth. Say to yourself, I exist in this world. I have a spark of life that's mine alone, a combination of genes, heritage, and life experiences unlike any other person on earth. I am unique, one of a kind in all of history. No one else can or will make the same contribution to the universe that I do. The universe would be a different place if I had not been born. I affect the lives of everyone I come into contact with. I have irreversibly altered the course of the universe by my presence, my children, my friendships, my life. Take time to consider the power of these words.

When you feel that you've plumbed the depth and the breadth of that thought, take the next step. Think to yourself, I have a right to be here. I did not ask to be born. I did not promise to meet anyone's expectations. I need not defend my existence here any more than the trees and the flowers and animals need to defend their existence here. I exist as a unique individual, placed here by forces beyond anyone's understanding. That's all that matters.

Finally, think to yourself, this is my life to live. I can pursue whatever I find meaningful. I need not live for the approval of other people. I need only live a life that makes me satisfied with myself, a life that includes goodness and honesty and integrity. The approval I've been seeking from others I must seek from myself.

Keep Your Focus

These are the concepts that lie at the very root of self-esteem. Once you grasp them, embrace them, and believe them, you're well on your way to a healthy view of self. And when something bad happens—like losing a job—they can help you avoid feelings of worthlessness.

Keep in mind that this is not an exercise to be performed just once or twice. On the contrary, especially in the critical emotional period just after a layoff, you may need to repeat this process many times. And depending on how often you battle feelings of worthlessness, it may help to take the exercise even further.

After more than two decades of psychiatric practice, I've come to believe that good people tend to focus mainly on what they consider their bad parts. It's as though they're looking at themselves with a distorted lens—a lens that magnifies supposed flaws and shrinks everything good and honorable. If you battle feelings of worthlessness, you're probably one of those good people looking through a distorted lens. By changing your lens, changing your focus, you can make yourself feel dramatically better. Here's how.

Virtually every person on earth has done good things. You're one of them. You've done plenty of positive, helpful things that enriched your life or the life of another person—things that, if you knew another person did them, would make you like and appreciate that person. Think about those things. Write them down. Then, when you start to think negative thoughts about yourself, make a conscious effort to replace those thoughts with the positive ones you've prepared. In the beginning, you may need to help distract yourself away from the negative thoughts so you can insert the positive ones. For example, you may want to wear a rubber band around your wrist. When feelings of worthlessness begin to rise, distract yourself from them by snapping the rubber band lightly against your wrist. That brief distraction may be all the time you need to inject positive thoughts consciously into your brain. Methods of distraction differ for every person. Maybe you'd prefer going for a quick walk, getting a drink of water, smelling the flowers in your yard, looking at a book filled with beautiful pictures. The technique is not the issue. The effect is the issue. Do whatever you need to do to help yourself quickly stop thinking about worthlessness and start thinking positive things about yourself.

Don't forget that your thoughts alter the chemistry in your brain. It's literally true that what you think affects who you are. If you need to, go back again to chapter 8 and reread the parts about brain chemistry. You'll affirm that you have the power to change the way you feel about yourself by consciously changing the way you think about yourself.

If you're one of those people for whom work wields a mighty influence on your feelings of self-worth, getting laid off may turn out to be the best thing that ever happened to you. It will feel terrible at first. But it may force you to realize that your job does not define your worth. As you work through the emotional pain of it all, you'll come to understand that your self-worth is a constant. It does not change with the vagaries of life's events or other people's thoughts.

Keep in mind that corporate America has entered a period of revolution directed not at individual workers but at the system as a whole. If you are in the line of fire, so to speak, your working life may have to change. But your intrinsic worth never will. Imagine it this way. Imagine driving down your street one day, only to discover that your family home has been hit by lightning and burned to the ground. Not many of life's events are more tragic than that. You feel shock. You grieve. You cry. You mourn. You curse the sky. But you don't turn it on yourself. You don't feel worthless and a failure because something bad happened to you that was outside your control. And what's happening in the American workplace is most definitely outside your control.

Also keep in mind that the longer you've worked for a company, the harder a layoff is likely to hit you. That's because the longer you identify with a particular employer, the more your self-esteem tends to get tangled up in that employer and its actions. If you're like Susan McGuire, and your main goal in life is business success, you're even more likely to fall into that category.

As Susan faithfully worked through these profound concepts with me, I started to notice a slight change in her. She began to lighten, to laugh. She began to see, over time, that she was a valuable human being, no matter where she worked or what salary she made. One day Susan said to me, "I think I confused my net-worth with my self-worth," and I knew she'd rounded the corner.

It's not easy to rebuild your sense of self-worth from the ground up. But healthy feelings of self-worth occupy a place at the center of the human soul. You'll be glad they're built on a solid foundation.

1 2

Mastering Monsters

SCHOLARS FROM EVERY DISCIPLINE tell us that rational thought is one of the hallmarks of humanity. Our ability to apply logic and reason to a myriad of situations makes us distinctively human. It sets us apart from what we know to be true about the earth's other animals. And it spurs us onward. Logic and reason lie at the base of fantastic human inventions and spectacular advances in science, culture, and technology. The truth is that we owe much of our advancement as a species to the blessing of rational thought.

But the blessing of rational thought can bring with it a curse as well, if we're not careful. It's a common human reaction. Because we're able to make sense of some situations, we want to make sense of *every* situation. We want to know the reasons for why things happen. We want to understand events as they unfold. We don't want to accept that something just *is*. And we certainly don't want to accept things we disagree with.

Here lies the source of the curse. For those of us fixated on making sense of all life's events, there's a real risk of creating a bitter and unhappy future. Why? Because it's easy to be beguiled by blame and envy. When something turns out differently than we wanted, it's easy to search for someone to blame. When people move ahead of us, especially if we can't see a good reason for it, it's easy to envy them their success. Examples abound in today's business world. Just walk

the halls of almost any corporation. Sit in the lunch room. Tour the
executive suite. You'll hear it inside and outside the company walls:
Former employees blaming executives for laying them off. Current
employees blaming managers for ever-increasing workloads. Managers envying the prosperity of the CEO and top executives. Executives blaming the managers and employees for spotty quality and a
lackluster effort.

The variety is so great that we tend to lump these reactions all together and call them *complaining*. But I think it's useful to be more
precise than that. It's useful for each of us to examine our relationship
with blame and envy, and to recognize the negative impact they have
on our lives.

The problem with blame and envy, as you'll see in this chapter, is
that they often have little to do with reality. They're based on a personal translation of situations that unfold around you—situations
about which you seldom have all the information, situations that you
typically can't change even if you want to. So blame and envy simply
lead you down a garden path to nowhere. In fact, indulging in them
is simply another way to waste your most valuable commodity: time.
If you insist on keeping company with blame and envy, if you can't
find a way to reach a state of acceptance, beware. You could end up
like Teresa Martinez.

No One Cared

On the phone before our first meeting, Teresa asked me if I could
help her with "an anger problem." I told her I'd be happy to see her
and, after hanging up, wondered for a moment what she meant by
that, and who she'd turn out to be. A week later, I opened my office
door to find a thin young woman with spiky auburn hair and enormous brown eyes. She wore trendy, slack-hanging clothes but no
jewelry, not even a watch. Her black combat boots made dull,
clumping sounds as she crossed the wood floor toward me. I guessed
that she hadn't yet turned 30.

I invited Teresa to take a seat and she did, crossing her legs so one boot dangled heavily, like an anchor, above the other. She pressed two straight fingers against her lips for a moment, as though she wished a cigarette were between them, then curled both hands in her lap. She looked thin-lipped and irritated, about what I couldn't speculate. But it didn't take long for her to fill me in.

Teresa told me that she needed help because she was afraid— afraid that the ceaseless anger she felt toward her former employer might push her into actions she couldn't control and might regret. She told me that she plotted revenge, that she couldn't stop fuming about how she'd been tricked by people she trusted. I asked her to tell me the whole story, starting at the beginning. So she did.

By the time she finished college, Teresa told me, she knew that she wanted to work in human resources. She liked the whole idea of it—helping other people make the most of their careers, helping a company find talented, motivated people, helping the corporate system run smoothly, based on policies that were fair and humane. And besides, she reasoned, an HR department isn't expendable. As long as you have employees, you need HR. It seemed like a safe choice with a supportive mission.

Smart and personable, Teresa didn't take long to find her first job. She joined a growing software company as HR associate. She and the director made up the entire department. But the way things were going, the director told her, it wouldn't be long before the company— and the department—doubled. That meant plenty of room for advancement. For a while, it seemed he was right. The company launched several successful software products. And it began adding divisions responsible for developing more. Before long, Teresa began hearing speculation that the company could go public. And then, just 18 months after Teresa started, her boss abruptly resigned to take a job with a competitor. Puzzled, she wondered why anyone would leave at a time filled with such great potential. She didn't worry about it for long, however, because much to her delight, Teresa was made acting HR director. She felt that she'd merged smoothly into the fast lane, that she'd "made it" in a company that was going places.

Two weeks later, the company announced that it had been pur-
chased by a multimedia giant. The company's young founders became instant millionaires. But many of the other employees weren't
so lucky. Over the course of the next six months, the new owner
made it clear that only the Internet division would survive unscathed.
Representatives from the new company told Teresa to shepherd the
other divisions through a drastic downsizing.

From the beginning of her brief career, Teresa had known that
she would have to participate in firing an employee from time to
time. She made herself feel better with the knowledge that termination was justified when a person did a poor job. But this was different. And it was agonizing. Teresa had to fire more than 100
intelligent, motivated people. People who were older than she was.
People who had been with the company since it started in a vacant
warehouse. People who had families and expectations of success with
their innovative employer. This was not Teresa's idea of human resources. She wanted to help people get ahead, not take their heads.
Feeling guilty and cruel, she did what the new owner asked of her.
She fired people while maintaining as much professionalism as she
could muster. And at the end of it all, the new owner fired her as
well, replacing her with one of its own employees.

Teresa got only two weeks of severance pay. But she found herself unable to look for a new job right away. Instead, she slept and
watched movies for nearly a week. At the video store one evening,
she ran into her old boss, who asked how she was doing. "Not great,"
she shrugged, and then told him he was lucky to have left when he
did. He looked at her, a little surprised, and said, "It wasn't luck. I
knew they were going to sell. And I knew they were going to use us
as the bad guys, then replace us with one of their own people as the
good guy. That's what they do."

Teresa was stunned. It had been a trick all along. None of them
had cared about her or the other employees. They just used her loyalty and good intentions to save themselves. All of them. Including
her old boss. And especially the new owner. She felt like a fool, a

lover duped by an unscrupulous mate. She was angry, and she couldn't let go. Unable to make peace with what they had done to her, Teresa was unable to get on with her life. She blamed them for their deception, her disappointment, and her humiliating need to stand in the unemployment line. And she blamed herself for being so naive.

Who's to Blame?

When something bad happens, you may find that your first reaction is to look for someone to blame. That's not because you're a bad person. It's because you want things to make sense. You want the world to be predictable and reliable and logical. You want your trust to be upheld. You want a sense of security. You want an outlet for the emotions raised by a disturbing event. The illusion is that if you can find someone to blame, then the bad thing can be undone and justice (your version of it, anyway) can be restored. If you can determine that someone did something wrong or evil, then theoretically you can get in there and change the situation, replace the person, undo the damage. If only you can find out who's to blame, this person or group then becomes the focus for your fear, rage, and self-hatred.

In general, this desire to blame doesn't work. It only fans the flames of personal unhappiness. At its extreme, it can lead to violence in society and in the workplace. How? The reasoning goes like this. If something bad happens that isn't my fault, then it must be someone else's fault. And if I can't find someone in particular to blame, then I'll find someone in general to blame. Maybe it's the blacks. The whites. The Jews. The gays. The Asians. The *other*. Whoever you can make into the other then becomes dehumanized enough to become the target for your emotions. This kind of thinking leads to irritability and needless combat in the community. We yell at other drivers and make obscene gestures from the anonymous safety of our cars. We wave guns at each other on the freeway. When taken to its logical conclusion, this kind of thinking can lead to very serious problems. Problems like the Holocaust. Gang violence. The growing hate-group movement in the United States. The Ku Klux Klan.

When you see it spelled out in black and white before you, it becomes obvious that this kind of thinking is pointlessly destructive. Of course it's not the blacks' fault. Of course it's not the Jews' fault. It's not the fault of any group. It's just that people sometimes try to place their emotions on someone else rather than addressing and working through them. Especially when the dominant culture is suffering, we risk the acceleration of these problems. That's because if, in your mind, you have to find someone to blame, you may be willing to create someone to blame. Instead of recognizing and working through your sadness about the unfairness of a situation, the tendency to blame simply pushes that sadness into rage. Sometimes that rage is translated into destructive behaviors, even murder.

The real answer here is to recognize our tendency to blame others, and stop it. The fact of the matter is that, in our current economic climate, there is no one to blame for our layoffs, our job insecurity, our stagnating wages. Certainly, there are always a few bad guys here and there. But basically, the issue is our economy. No one can magically restore it to its post–World War II heyday. When you think about the Great Depression, can you find someone to blame for it? Of course not. Trying to find someone is simply a waste of time. Like then, we are now in a period of historical change. It's like being out on the sea in a boat when a storm comes up. That a storm happened to come up in the midst of your journey is no one's fault. But you still have to steer your way through it.

Liberating Feeling

So who have you been spending your energy blaming? I hear a lot of people blaming the CEOs. They're ordering all the layoffs while lining their pockets with millions of dollars. Okay, let's say that the CEOs are greedy and it's their fault. And let's say that we could take all their money away from them and distribute it to all the workers. Do you think that would solve the problem? No, it wouldn't. It might feel better momentarily, but it would not solve the problem. In fact, even though some CEOs may be greedy, even though they may be getting more than their "fair" (there's that word again) share, that is unrelated to the real problem. It's not the main reason why you're not making a higher wage. The real problem is the reduced growth rate and global competition we've been experiencing in our economy.

Now, just for a moment, imagine that you acted on your feelings. Imagine that you shot the person that's theoretically to blame for your layoff. It's not going to do a thing for you except put you in prison where you'll be no good to yourself or your family. If your reaction is, "Of course I wouldn't shoot anyone," let me ask you this. Are you spending time thinking about shooting someone? Are you spending time thinking about scraping a key down the side of someone's car? Are you spending time thinking about sabotaging someone's computer, writing exposé letters to the newspaper, giving that person a piece of your mind? If you are spending your mental energy *at all* on the person you think is to blame for your predicament, you're in the same boat with the shooter. You just won't get the jail time. Anger kills, literally. And you may end up with high blood pressure, a heart attack, or other potentially life-threatening problems to show for it.

Keep in mind that human logic is based largely on cause and effect. It makes us uncomfortable to think that something just *is*. It makes us feel powerless, and that's a very scary feeling. But we have to get used to it. Some things just *are*. If you're willing to accept the notion that we are indeed powerless to control everything, it can be very liberating. You don't have to blame any more. You don't have to spin your wheels trying to make sense of every event that occurs in your life. As religious people say, you can "let go and let God." Really, what alternative do you have? It's a waste of your mental energy to search continually for someone to blame. Remember that you only get a certain amount of that mental energy. Why spend it on people who aren't helping you solve your problem? It's a much better—more adaptive—solution to use your mental energy to find good solutions and a good future for you and your family.

Forget about blaming someone else. Instead, help yourself expel that anger through exercise, meditation, or another healthy method.

Try to accept the apparent randomness of events. Or believe that, if events are controlled by a divine power, they're too complex for us to understand. This way, you can free yourself to accept unforeseen events rather than stoking your anger by blaming others. For example, say you don't get into the college you want. But you do get into a "lesser" one and there you meet the person of your dreams. It turned out to be a good thing, didn't it? But you'll never know which option would have been better for you in the long run. It's the road not taken. Likewise with your job, you'll never know whether losing a job was better for you in the long run, because you don't know what would have happened had you kept the job. Maybe the ceiling would have fallen in over your desk and flattened you. Maybe someone would have walked into your office and shot everyone in sight. Maybe the company president would have come to your desk and tapped you to be the next vice president. Who knows? You don't. So there's no use blaming someone else for the events that happen in your life, or wasting your time regretting them. They're going to happen. You can choose how to handle them.

So what can you do with all the emotion you've tried to foist off on someone else? Get it out in a healthy way. Do something for yourself. Get some exercise. Talk to people you trust. Just talking can provide a tremendous relief. Then turn all that energy and emotion toward problem-solving. Take that energy and throw it into improving your body and improving your mind. Then you can work on finding logical solutions instead of finding someone to blame.

Forgive Yourself

For many of the patients I see, blaming others isn't their biggest problem. Rather, they tend to blame *themselves* any time something goes wrong, even if it wasn't their fault. This is especially common among people who battle with low self-esteem. That's a huge pool of people. Maybe you're one of them. Maybe you're asking yourself those "if only" questions outlined in chapter 8. Maybe you feel you should have seen your layoff coming. Maybe you wish you had worked harder, smarter, faster so you wouldn't have lost your job. The types of torture you can put yourself through are almost endless.

This kind of torture will not help you. If you're laid off in today's economic climate, chances are that there's no reason to blame yourself for it. You're simply spinning your wheels as I described in the last section, only this time you're turning the anger and hatred directly on yourself instead of looking for someone else to blame. The core issue remains: accepting and adapting to an unpredictable world. It doesn't help to blame others. It surely doesn't help to blame yourself.

I realize that this is easier said than done. If you're blaming yourself for losing your job, how can you stop? There are several ways. Start by forgiving yourself. Look at all the people who have lost their jobs. They number in the millions. They can't all be bad workers. In fact, very few of them are bad workers. But the goals of their companies have changed around them. You're probably in the same boat. Why shouldn't you assume that a large portion of your job loss stems directly from what's been happening in the economy? That's not your fault. If you were a railroad worker when the airplane replaced the railroad, would it be your fault that you lost your job? No. You may be a great railroad worker. But if the economy changes directions, you could lose your job anyway.

Another way to stop blaming yourself is to concentrate on the skills that will get you your next job. Think about how the skills you developed in your last job will help you find another one. Maybe those skills need some updating. Maybe they need some enhancement. But it's better to spend your time figuring out how to do that than berating yourself. It's difficult to start again. But when you're willing to adapt and push yourself to move on, it gives you a chance to learn new skills, to prove to yourself that you can still grow and learn. Not that you would have wished a layoff on yourself, of course. But you can make yourself better because of it. And in that process of making yourself better, you'll reduce the tendency to blame yourself for things that aren't your fault.

Even recognizing that you *did* have something to do with your layoff can be helpful. Say you didn't do such a great job. You slacked a bit. At the time you were doing that, was everyone else doing it too? Were you performing to the average level? Maybe what we'd consider slacking now was a typical work day in the early or mid '80s. Don't forget that you have to consider events in their context. There was a time when the most fashionable men wore long curly wigs. It would look ridiculous now, but it was appropriate then. You shouldn't blame yourself as much if you were with the times.

The bottom line is this. If you recognize that your performance had something to do with your layoff, good. You recognized it. Once you recognize it, you can do something about it. Now that the work world has become more competitive, you'll rise to the occasion. Maybe there wasn't a need for you to rise to the occasion before. You didn't know these economic changes were coming. Blaming yourself for losing your job is just Monday-morning quarterbacking. It's a waste of energy. Put that energy into what you can do now to help yourself and others. Learn from history, don't do it again, and move on. It's harder to blame yourself when you're moving forward, looking ahead instead of taking potshots at yourself.

A Partial Picture

For most of us, blame goes hand in hand with envy. This makes sense. First you try to pin blame on someone for your unhappy circumstances. Then you look at someone else's life and wish you could change places. If you could only change places, you think, it would get you out of your unhappy circumstances. This is envy. You're saying, "I wish I had what you have." This reaction is common and understandable to some extent. But if you give in to it, if you're consumed by it, you'll once again be wasting that precious mental energy on an illusion.

Why is it an illusion? Because you can't possibly see inside another person's life. You can see that person's reality only as you observe it from the outside. Then your imagination fills in the rest. And imaginations are never accurate. When you envy someone else, you don't see the whole picture. Here's an example. I have a patient who greatly envied a friend who bought a new Porsche. So I made a hypothetical proposal. Say you could have her Porsche, I suggested. But you'd have to take her breast cancer too. And you'd have to take the husband who abandoned her because of the breast cancer. Okay, now you have more of the picture. Do you still want to change places with this woman?

It's impossible to understand someone else's reality. All you can do is try to deal with your own. We are all confronted with our own journey, our own field to plow. Some of that field will be rough and rocky. You'll sweat and get frustrated. Some of it will be deep, rich earth, satisfying and productive. But looking at someone else's journey and thinking you can know what it's like is a mistake. You can't.

It's not your fault if you're hung up in envy. Our culture encourages it, thrives on it. In some ways, our society revolves around cultivating envy. We see the messages every day. If you drive this luxury car, you'll be powerful and sexy and smart. If you weigh 100 pounds, you'll be beautiful and sexy and rich. After hearing these messages constantly, who could be immune? So if your next-door neighbor gets a brand new car, a shiny new gas grill, a souped up new computer, suddenly your stuff doesn't look so good any more. Suddenly your reliable but dented car isn't good enough. The gas grill you've cooked masterpieces on looks grimy and rusted. The computer you've used happily for three years suddenly requires the patience of Job. So you have to go out and buy new stuff, probably using loans or credit cards, to try to make yourself feel better. Look carefully at this situation and ask yourself who benefits the most. It's the sellers of cars, gas grills, and computers. They have to sell products to keep

their businesses alive. Creating a sense of need and envy in their potential buyers is a great way to keep those sales rolling in.

You don't have to be one of those buyers. You don't have to let
yourself get caught up in a system that doesn't care if you spend too
much money or go too far into debt. I don't know who printed the
bumper sticker that says "He who dies with the most toys wins," but
it must have been someone selling something. Especially if you've
lost a job or you think you might lose it, subscribing to this philosophy can be disastrous. Because he who dies with the most toys won't
win anything except the biggest bills.

Don't misunderstand me. I'm not trying to undermine people
who make things and sell them. That's the system that makes our
economy work, and I wouldn't want to change it. What I am trying
to do is help you see that envy is the wrong reason for buying something. Does it really matter what kind of car you drive? It matters
who's in the car with you. It matters that the car is safe. But the kind
of car you drive can be worse than meaningless. It can mean something to you as a status symbol. And it's just packaging.

I know a woman who got out of her Mercedes carrying a Louis
Vuitton bag and looked across the street at another woman who was
also getting out of a Mercedes and carrying a Louis Vuitton bag. For
a moment, she envied that woman. And then, with the force of a slap
in the face, she realized what she was doing. She was so busy scanning
her environment for what she didn't have that she lost sight of what
she did have. She laughs about it now, but she also says she'll never
forget that lesson.

This story illustrates very well that envy can get a grip on you no
matter what your financial status, no matter how much you have or
don't have. Don't fool yourself by saying, "If only I could get that car,
then I'd have enough." You won't. If you're driven by what other
people have, you'll never have enough. Someone will always have
more. You have to get down to the bedrock truth. And the truth that
I've seen in patient after patient over the years is this: Satisfaction in
life does not come from getting the right stuff. It comes from being

satisfied with what you have. It comes from shifting your priorities off of your stuff and onto your spouse, your family, your good friends, your efforts to help people who need it, your ability to be creative in whatever you do—things that really are important.

If you have a problem with envy, don't blame or berate yourself for it. It's a natural reaction, given the society we live in. But you can start to wean yourself away from it. Start by staying away from places that are filled with stuff you think you want or that society encourages you to want. Sit down and think about what's really important to you. Think of it this way. If you suddenly had to flee to another country and you could choose only six things to take with you, what would they be? They probably wouldn't be things at all. You'd probably take your spouse, your kids, your most loved friend, maybe a pet, pictures or other memories. You get the idea. Decide what's really important to you. What are the core things? Then concentrate on being grateful for them, cultivating them, thinking about them. Cultivate a sense of good fortune for what you have in your life. And never forget that, even if someone else's life looks better than yours, you don't know the whole picture, past, present, and future. You don't even know your own picture, and what wonderful things may be in store for you.

13

Attitude Alters the Facts

AYBE IT'S A CONDITION of human life that we're unable to see the big picture at all times. Maybe the big picture is simply *too* big for us to grasp with one sweeping turn of the head. I don't know. What I do know is that, in general, we humans have the ability to choose which parts of the picture to focus on. What you choose makes all the difference in what you see of the world, and what you believe about how life is likely to treat you.

What you choose to focus on has a direct relationship to the attitude you develop about the future, other people, your work, adversity—literally everything. Your attitude, in turn, has a direct relationship to the quality and maybe even the quantity of your life. Your attitude colors your interpretation of everything that happens to you or doesn't happen to you. It deeply affects your relationships with other people. It alters the way you feel and the way you think. It influences your level of success. It may even affect your physical health. Attitude truly is everything.

Over and over, we see motivated, optimistic people beat the odds. People with incurable cancers get better. People who face terrible tragedies go on to develop wisdom and grace. People with daunting disabilities find ways to overcome. In some cases, it seems that attitude alters the facts. But even when these people don't beat the odds, their optimistic, positive attitudes result in a better life, whatever life brings. In *your* life too, your attitude is largely your choice. That's not to say the choice is always easy. It may not even be apparent, at the time. But the fact remains that attitude is one of the things you can—and should—control. By doing so, you may find yourself more satisfied and content than ever.

Attitude Adjustment

Imagine, for a moment, two people who live in the same town and work for the same employer some 20 miles away. They drive the same congested road to work. And they know that, on some days, they'll spend time sitting in traffic. On those days, person #1 fusses and fumes, rants at the other drivers, races the engine, and changes lanes at every opportunity just to get one car length closer to work. Person #2 uses the delay to make lists, listen to music, have a conversation, plan an upcoming trip. This person almost looks forward to the delay because it offers a little extra time to think and get organized. It's like forced free time. I can virtually guarantee that, despite all the revving and raving, person #1 will arrive at work scant minutes ahead of person #2. I can also guarantee that person #1 will be having a really bad day when he or she gets there. Same day. Same road. Different attitude.

Here's another example. I have a kind and capable patient named Beverly who has been overweight all her life. At 5'4", Beverly weighs something over 200 pounds. This extra weight affects her job performance not at all. But it does, at times, affect her attitude about herself. That's why, when Beverly got a job at a large utility company some 20 years ago, she never forgot a comment made by her new boss. After a drink or two at a company party, the boss informed Beverly that, "no fatso makes it up the ladder here, so you better not set your sights on this company for a future." At the time, this cruel comment only drove Beverly on to prove herself. She worked hard, did well, and got ahead. Despite her boss's prediction, Beverly did climb the ladder, all the way up to regional vice president. But recently, at 55 years old, Beverly got laid off in a massive, company-wide downsizing move. And now she struggles with that comment her boss made two decades ago. One day, after the layoff, she said to me, "I guess my boss was right. I couldn't make it in that company." I nearly came out of my chair to disagree with her. Beverly was using faulty reasoning. By anyone's standards, she *did* make it at that company. She stayed longer and rose higher than literally thousands of other people who worked there. But she was choosing not to look at it that way.

So much in life depends on how you see things. We're all looking at the same big picture, but we each tune into different views of it. And in general, what you focus on is what you get. If you're expecting to see trouble, you'll probably find some of it to focus on. If you're expecting good fortune, you'll probably find some of that to focus on.

Chin Up

In this unpredictable world, at this time when work is a major source of anxiety, I think one of the most important things you can do for yourself is to be an optimist. I firmly believe that it's better to be an optimist and be wrong than a pessimist and be right. Why? Because although the outcome may be the same, the optimist will have lived a better life. And that's what it's all about, isn't it? An optimist is a person who assumes and expects that, eventually, something positive will come out of a situation, even a negative situation. And by focusing on that probability of a positive outcome, the optimist is more likely to see it or create it.

Everyone arrives at optimism through a slightly different door. For some, a certain degree of resilience and positive thinking are genetically programmed. Looking at the bright side is such a person's default, as it were. Other people learn optimism as children, from parents or other important adults. Still others find optimism only by passing through some of life's most difficult circumstances. Consider my friend Rosemary, who, frankly, spent a good portion of her time complaining. Then she was diagnosed with a rare and aggressive form of cancer. Rosemary knew that she would die. In the harsh light of her dire circumstances, suddenly Rosemary could see how important it is to be grateful for a typical, everyday life, even if that life encounters difficult and trying events from time to time (and what life doesn't?). Rosemary found herself wondering—out loud—why we don't get up each morning saying, "Wow. I'm alive. I'm healthy. I can do a good day's work. I care about someone in my life. I was born in the most wonderful country in the world." Instead, she observed, we complain and minimize what we have until we encounter a real threat that it could be taken away. Then we realize how much we've had all along. If only we could come to that realization sooner.

Fortunately, you can, because optimism can be learned. Even if your natural inclination is to dwell on the dark side of life, you can help yourself be more optimistic. In fact, in my opinion, you *have* to be as optimistic as possible if you want to live with some semblance of satisfaction in this world. If you want to become more optimistic, keep these few things in mind, not necessarily in this order. First, don't blame and berate yourself that you're not more optimistic! Second, be open to the very positive effect that humor can have on your life, your attitude, and your health. Don't create humor at someone else's expense, of course. Just find a way to do some good old-fashioned laughing. Third, if you're having trouble with your attitude, try a little attitude adjustment. Intentionally shift your energy away from negative or destructive thoughts and toward something that's good for you and other people. Get excited. Get moving. Start a new hobby or take a fun class. Try charity. Go and help someone else. That's a great way to stop thinking about yourself. Go to a soup kitchen or help out with a food bank. Not to minimize your legitimate concerns, but, go find out how good you really have it. Fourth, get some exercise. Vigorous physical activity releases endorphins that, without any other help, can alter your mood. Plus, exercise is an adaptive way to drain yourself of stress and anger.

Finally, make a conscious effort to begin talking differently to yourself. Where learning optimism is concerned, it's okay to fake it 'til you make it. Start by taking care of reasonable contingencies, of course. But then adopt the thought that, since life is totally unpredictable, you might as well assume the positive. Then do what you can to slant things toward the positive. It's best to think that, if you act responsibly and do what you can, things in general will work out better for you. Take all the forces in your environment and use them to create the good thing that's going to come next, even if what's coming next doesn't look like a very good thing. The other day I called a psychiatrist friend of mine who was going through a particularly hard time and said, "How are you doing?" He replied, "I'm dancing on the Titanic!" If you know the boat is going to sink, what else can you do? You might as well dance. Unquestionably, this is not an easy mind-set to attain. But you can do it if you concentrate on the positive aspect, if you focus on your assets. You can do it if you're willing to be an optimist.

A Habit of Mind

It goes almost without saying that losing your job can do a real number on your attitude. That's to be expected. But if you can find a way to be an optimist, the worst of the negative effects will be temporary. If you insist on sitting down in the disaster, however, its negative effects may surround you for years, even a lifetime. It seems well worth your while to look for the potential good side. Maybe your layoff will provide the impetus you needed to reevaluate yourself and what you think about the world. After all, it seems that moments of crisis can bring mountains of revelation.

As I've said before, if you lose your job, the best thing to do is cry.

Let it out somehow. Think about what you've lost and accept it as a sad thing. In any crisis, layoff included, you're going to experience a period of mourning. The length of that mourning period is a little different for each person. If you lost a job you held for 20 years, for example, you're probably going to need a significant period of mourning—significantly longer than someone who held the job for only a couple of years. Eventually, however, you can begin to tell yourself that you can handle this. Even if you're not 100 percent convinced of it, you can tell yourself that whatever happens, you'll find a way to handle it, get through it, and come out the other side with your mental and physical health intact. If you can say that to yourself, you're very likely to be right.

I have a friend who, if his house were falling down around him, would probably be able to look up at the California hills and say, "Aren't we in a beautiful place?" This may sound a little extreme, and perhaps it is. But he grew up in the Bronx housing projects and he has somehow found a way to keep that contrast in the front of his mind. Most people forget what they have. It's a habit of mind to make yourself travel quickly back over your life and realize that you have much to be grateful for, even if some things aren't going quite right just now.

This habit is, in large part, the source of a great well of resilience: to be able to look back on what you've handled in the past and, because of it, believe that you can handle what will come at you in the future. Virtually everyone has experienced difficulty earlier in life. Scan back over your years and you may hear yourself saying, "I *did* handle it when I had to repeat calculus. I *did* handle it when my first wife left me. I *did* handle it when my house caught fire. I *did* handle it when my second son was born deaf." The list is endless and, obviously, different for each person. And by saying that you handled something, you're definitely not saying that it was easy. The purpose of the exercise is to look at those difficult things, situations that you thought might destroy you or ruin what you built, and believe that if you could get through them, you can get through this too. And as I've said before, in this day and age, you don't need to be overly critical of yourself for losing your job. There's no reason to see yourself as a loser. In this situation, there's no reason to struggle against yourself.

As difficult as your circumstances can be, your inner peace does not have to be destroyed by them. The rapid changes we're going through just now don't have to change your sense of optimism. You can still keep the feeling that you'll be able to get through these changes, whatever they turn out to be, and come up in a good position. If you're like most people, you have a pretty good track record of getting through difficult things. Some take longer than others. But you've probably come through a lot in your life. That ability will work for you again. You may even find yourself thinking, as plenty of people do, "I never have been able to find the gumption to leave this dead-end job on my own. I'm actually thankful that the company gave me the kick in the behind I needed to get moving."

What's your option, after all? Your employer may be able to take your job away from you, but fortunately in this country, you still own your body and your mind. So you still have what got you your last job. And that leads me to believe that, if you're willing to continue to use your body and your mind to their best abilities, you can find a way to get another job. You may make less money. You may need to change your lifestyle. But you'll be okay. Just for a moment, think about your worst-case scenario. What is it? Maybe you'll have to live in a smaller house or apartment. Maybe you'll drive an older car. But unless you are mentally or physically ill, the chances that you'll risk starvation are very slim indeed.

If you compare your worst-case scenario and your best-case scenario, you'll realize that there's lots of room between them for a perfectly happy life, as long as you don't base your self-esteem on labels and things. You can sit and dwell forever on thoughts like, "I worked 10 years to afford my BMW, and now I can't afford it any more." Or, "I worked hard to have this big house, and now I may have to sell it." Or, "I put all my effort into this job, and now I'm out." This kind of thinking will only prolong your agony. It simply won't help. And besides, what you don't know is that maybe this is your chance to become something else. Maybe this is your chance to jump to a new place in life. Maybe this is your chance.

The Best Revenge

We've seen over and over now that there's no such thing as guaranteed job security. In fact, the only real security you have is your attitude about things. You can't change what's happening to you. What you can change is how you react to it. It may not be a snap. But it's the only really changeable thing that you have complete control over. Maybe gaining that control is easier than you think.

Imagine yourself reading a book or watching a movie. You're deeply involved in the story and concentrating on the plot line and the action happening before you. The more you allow yourself to become involved in the story, the more you feel as though you're actually there, inside the story. You're not, obviously. You're still sitting in the same chair you were before. But it *feels* like you're in a different place, like you're in whatever place the story is unfolding. You can go so far away in your mind that you may not even hear someone enter and leave the room. If the human mind can do this just by scanning the pages of a book or watching movement on a screen, I know that you can use your mental powers to help yourself when you really need it. Your mind can help you change your mind about seeing the positive aspects of every situation.

I can hear some of you saying, "I've been the way I am for years now. If I could change my attitudes, I would have done it by now. I just can't." Baloney. I don't believe in "can't." I do believe, however, that as long as you *say* "I can't," you'll be right. The trick is to convince yourself to start saying "I can" every so often. Lo and behold, you'll find that you're still right. But now you're building a better mind-set, with a more promising outcome. In some ways, it may be frightening to become more optimistic. Or maybe you still feel too angry to let go of those negative feelings. Go ahead. Get good and angry. Let it out. Rant and rave. Do whatever you have to do. But then make the decision that, if your employer has done you in, you're not going to allow it to continue by wasting more energy on what they did to you. If you want to help your enemies, if you have them or think you have them, you're certainly on your way to doing it if you stay stuck in anger. Besides holding you captive to negative attitudes, hanging onto anger can wreak havoc in your body. Continuous anger affects your immune system, makes you more vulnerable to diseases, alienates the people who want to help you. You'll use up all your energy on anger so you don't have any left for constructive purposes. Then you'll become a worse enemy to yourself than the people who took your job were to you.

Thinking about things this way is something of an indirect method to help you see what you're doing to yourself. It's not to say that I think you should dwell on your enemies, real or fabricated. In fact, living well is still the best revenge. And that doesn't mean just financial. It also means in your personal life, your inner peace, your relationships, and last but not least, your attitudes. If you find that you can't navigate this complex emotional transition on your own, there are plenty of places to get help. Try a professional, a peer group, a work group, whatever makes you feel most comfortable. The goal is to move on, to work through that anger and negative attitude and look toward a future that seems bright even if you can't see what's up ahead. After all, that's what being an optimist is all about.

| 4

<hr>

It's Not Over Yet

THERE'S SOMETHING OF A TRICK you can use to help yourself live as an optimist, a secret that can keep you going in the most trying of times. It's simple. But, like many simple concepts, it can have a powerful influence on your life, if you let it. The concept is this: It's not over until it's over. And it's not over yet.

Thinking like this can help you take the long view of your situation, whatever it is. Why does that help? Because if you're in an unpleasant situation, taking the long view can give you the stamina to weather it. After all, it can't last forever, right? On the other hand, if you're in a surprisingly pleasant situation, taking the long view will keep you from getting rigidly attached to it, unable to adapt to change. After all, even the best situation may not last forever, right?

Just pick your head up from whatever situation you're focused on at the moment and you'll see that the future is always up there, stretched out in front of you. You never get there. You don't know what's coming over the next bit of horizon. Or the one after that. So, until your life is over, it's never over. If you find yourself without a job and struggling to be motivated in your search for another, take heart. If you have a job but you're stressed or unhappy in it, take heart. This difficult period of your life won't last forever. If you look at the horizon and keep going on your journey, doing what you need to do, making the most of what you have, the scenery will change before you know it. And your attitude will change too.

Here are a few thoughts culled from what you've read so far that I think are especially helpful in taking the long view of our workplace worries. Try to hold these thoughts all in your mind at once, even if some of them seem to conflict. Make a list if you need to. And keep moving forward into your future.

You Are Not Your Job

If you want to weather what's happening in today's workplace, there's one thing about which you must be very clear. I've said this before and I'll say it again. You are not your job. I don't care what you do, whether you're a neurosurgeon, a social worker, a nuclear physicist, a plumber, a nurse, a bartender, an architect, a teacher, a salesperson, or Einstein himself. Do not equate yourself with your job. So many people lose sight of the distinction between who we are and what we do. This should come as no surprise, given that polite conversation in our society starts with, "What's your name?" and "What do you do?" After a while the two concepts seem conjoined—who I am and what I do. I *am* a middle manager. I *am* a corporate accountant. I *am* the boss's secretary. But thinking this way is wrong and, in our current predicament, it's dangerous too. Because if you lose your job, who are you? And if you don't know who you are, who can you become? See the danger?

Your job is not who you are. Your job is only one part of you. It's something you do. But there are lots of other things you do as well. You grow flowers. You express love to another person. You watch whales. You cook Chinese food. You have interests and pursuits specific to you. So not only is your job *not* who you are, it's only *one* of the things you do. In some moments it's the most important thing you do. In other moments it's the least important thing you do.

This is one of the crucial keys to taking the long view of our job crisis. You are not what you do. In fact, your job and the money you earn need not be the most important thing in your life or your loved ones' lives. Maybe the ideas, the humor, the friends, the love you bring into the house are more important than the money you bring home. Maybe assisting in the growth of a child—another human being—is more important than the money you bring home. It's all up to you. But if you want your job to play a healthy role in your life and your future, you have to be willing to look at yourself and the things you take as *given*. You have to be willing to reject the notion that the more powerful your job and the bigger your salary, the more important you are and the more respect you deserve. Take time regularly to think about what your job is in your life and what it isn't, what it should be and what it shouldn't be. You are not your job and your job is not you, no matter what you do for a living. By thinking this way, if you lose your job, you won't lose yourself too.

Your Job Matters

Okay, so you're not your job. And work is just one of the things you do. But to be satisfied with your life over the long haul, you should recognize and accept that work *is* important. A job is not just a job. Your job is your most tangible tie to the real world. You have to get up and go. You have to get dressed. You have to do something. Your job calls you to come outside of yourself. And it gives you rewards. You get paid for the work you do. Sometimes it's in money. Sometimes it's in gratitude. Sometimes it's in trade. Sometimes it's in self-satisfaction. There are lots of ways you can be rewarded by your work. But usually, you're compensated in some way that makes doing your work "worth it."

Your job probably also forms the structure of your daily patterns. It gives you a certain routine that anchors you to your life. You get up, you bathe, you brush your teeth, you make coffee, you make sure your clothes are clean and pressed. You pick out a tie or a pin that accents your clothes and expresses your style. You look forward to the funny stories your office mate is sure to tell about his weekend. You wonder if the person down the hall will flirt with you today. This is all healthy and normal and, to some degree, necessary for a contented life. We all want a purpose. A job is one important element of that purpose. You have a job that is valuable and needed and you're doing it and getting paid for it. This is good. You can respect yourself and others can respect you.

For all these reasons, work has a legitimate role in mental health. Don't try to minimize the importance of your job simply because it happens to be difficult right now, or because you don't have a job right now. Doing so will damage your self esteem, reduce your motivation, or both. Instead, find ways to replace the roles typically filled by your job. Or better yet, try to find a job that fits your needs and desires. This can be scary, I know. And if you have a harried home life besides, the thought of launching a job search can be daunting. You'd be surprised at the number of people who can't quit their jobs, even when they hate them, unless forced to. But you deserve to have a job that uses and builds your skills, gives you a sense of purpose, and rewards you for a job well done. If you don't have that, don't let fear stop you from trying to get it. Lift your eyes from the unhappy place you're in now, whether it's jobless or in a job you hate, and take the long view. Doing your best to find a fulfilling job can only help you in the long run.

By the way, don't forget to take the long view of that word "fulfilling" too. If you have a job you don't find inherently fulfilling, or you can't find one that is, maybe you need to alter your definition temporarily. Maybe you can find fulfillment in helping to support your family. Maybe you can find fulfillment in parts of your job, if not its entirety. And maybe you can find fulfillment by taking pride in doing the very best you can at whatever job you have.

Everything Changes

One of the most helpful things about taking the long view of life is that it tends to smooth out the feeling of being on a roller-coaster ride. From a distance, you can't feel the ups and downs as vividly as you can when you're poised at the crest of the hill, looking into the abyss. Imagine yourself on that roller coaster for a moment. What's the scariest part of the ride? For most people, it's when you first begin to roll down the biggest hill, and it's too late to turn back. That's a little bit like what has happened in the American workplace, only workers are not in an amusement park. This is for real. The people who experience the very first wave of changes, the first realization that we're beginning to go a different direction—at dizzying speeds— are the people affected most profoundly by the change. Once you're moving, whizzing along the tracks, it's not so scary.

That's why many younger people, in their 20s mostly, aren't as fazed by what the workplace offers these days. They don't expect to have one job for life. They don't expect loyalty from an employer. They have no reason to expect it, because many of these changes had already happened by the time they boarded the roller coaster.

Eventually, you get used to it. But in the beginning, when those changes are first beginning, it can be very disconcerting. Perhaps that's one reason why we resist change, why we always have inertia to overcome. Maybe it's easier—and less scary—to stay put instead of gathering enough energy to start moving in our own new direction. And herein lies a problem. When we're in that state of inertia, we tend not to look at our values very often. We tend not to evaluate whether we're really satisfied with our jobs and our performance in them.

So it seems there's some good news buried in all these workplace worries. Loss of your job is an opportunity that you would not have wished upon yourself, of course. But the gift it gives you is an unavoidable opportunity to reassess, to get off automatic pilot and start steering your own life again, to think about what you're doing. Losing your job gives you a chance to be in control again, even though the illusion is that you completely lost control. Too many of us establish a pattern of getting up in the morning, going to work, struggling through it, and coming home—only to do the same thing tomorrow, and tomorrow, and tomorrow, without really thinking about where all those tomorrows are leading.

This is the optimist's way of looking at job loss. It's an example of taking the long view. It's the belief that the loss of your job may allow you to change in incredibly new ways. Maybe your avocation will become your vocation. Maybe you'll be forced to learn new skills. Maybe you'll simply come to a new understanding that you can't avoid change in your life. But by taking the long view, you'll be better able to cope with that change and adapt to the new things it brings your way.

Nothing's Really New

More than 100 years ago, a physician named George Beard got interested in what he called "nervous disorders" and their causes. In Beard's day, there were no computers, no fax machines, no pagers (digital or otherwise), no modems, no airplanes, and no cars. The telephone and the lightbulb had barely been invented. It's hard to imagine a time more different than the one we live in today. So guess what Dr. Beard identified as the major causes of anxiety and mental health problems in his day? Take a look.

- The tyranny of time
- The speed at which information flows
- The rapid emergence and adoption of new ideas
- The jangling effect of noise on the nerves
- The anxiety of high-speed travel
- The increasing volume of business
- The tendency to ignore emotions
- Money trouble and domestic strife

Amazing, isn't it? If you didn't know when this list was made, you could assume that it referred to conditions as we know them right now. In fact, Dr. Beard's list cited the railroad as a means of high-speed travel and the telegraph as a conveyor of ideas. But if you simply replace some of his words and concepts with contemporary ones, it's obvious that we're still struggling with the same things.

It seems quite clear. The more things change, the more they stay the same. As shocked and dismayed as we are at what's happening to

American workers, we are not the first group of people to feel that the world as we know it is coming to an end. For decades and centuries, people have had fears of the same magnitude as ours. And yet, even though the world as they knew it has come to an end many times before, it's never come to an end. There's still a future. There's still a long view.

Enjoy What You Have

The best way to damage your future happiness is to dwell on your disappointing past. If you or a loved one has lost a job, try not to dwell on what you lost. Think about what you still have, and what you will have in the future. If you're like most people, that's a lot: your health, your spirituality, family, friends, social contacts, enjoyable sources of physical exercise, personal hobbies and interests, talents, and untapped potential. If you don't think you have any of those things, especially in this day and age, you'd better get some. If you do have them, take care to nurture them. You don't know what's around the next bend in the road. You don't know whether your situation will get better or worse. In either case, your ability to focus on the good things in your life can, over the long haul, make or break you.

Consider this story. Imagine a tiger chasing a Zen monk through the forest. The monk reaches the edge of a cliff and realizes that he'll have to climb down to keep from being eaten by the tiger. He begins to climb and, part way down, notices that another tiger awaits him at the bottom. So he scrambles to a nearby ledge. While sitting there, realizing that he can go neither forward nor back, he discovers a bush laden with lovely purple berries. Famished, he puts a berry in his mouth and discovers that it's delicious. The monk enjoys his berries one by one all through the night, knowing that they may be his last. As the sun begins to rise the following morning, the monk looks up to discover the tiger's glowing yellow eyes still trained on him. But as luck would have it, the tiger below him has vanished. So he climbs safely to the bottom of the cliff and continues on his journey.

What can modern Americans take from this story? Several things. Most important is that, even given the worst of all possible scenarios, your best option is to enjoy what you have. What's your alternative, after all? Blaming, complaining, and wishing you were elsewhere will only waste whatever time and energy you have. If you're lucky, maybe your situation will present you with opportunities, as in this monk's case. But you can't count on it. As far as you know, all you really have is this moment. So you might as well enjoy it.

Perhaps this story involves a monk because experiencing enjoyment despite difficult circumstances requires some ability to detach from yourself, to separate yourself from your seemingly dire straits and decide what's really best for you. Certainly, self-destruction is not the answer. Our monk could have decided he had no alternatives and flung himself to the waiting tiger. Fortunately, he chose a more self-sustaining path. Perhaps he realized that, for all of us, life begins with birth and ends with death. All you can do in the middle is the best you can to make the best of your life. You can either kick and scream all the way down, or you can enjoy yourself. Unlike the monk in our story, most Americans have a great deal to be thankful for and a great deal to enjoy. Unfortunately, however, many of us lack the wisdom to focus on and enjoy our relative riches. So who has the better life? The monk, who appreciates and enjoys what he has despite his circumstances, or modern-day Americans, who tend to concentrate on what we *don't* have? Not much of a contest, is it?

Take Your Opportunity

In these days of workplace anxiety and tumult, one of the surprising things you can enjoy—if you let yourself—is the time you're forced to spend reevaluating your future, taking the long view of your life and where it's going. Try to come at this with the spirit of an explorer going on an adventure. You know, so many of us don't have a minute left at the end of the day to relax or think or reflect. I see this in my patients all the time, and sometimes even in myself. Our culture places such a heavy emphasis on accomplishment that we tend to wear ourselves out just getting things done. We succumb to the tyranny of the urgent rather than going after what's really important for health and happiness.

So if you find yourself jobless, with some forced free time on your hands, realize that you've been given a gift, an opportunity to reconsider your direction in life. You'll be nervous about the lost income and a little battered by it all, of course. But try to remove yourself from those feelings for a while and just spend time thinking. Start with your self-concept. Who was I? Who am I? Who am I becoming? Who do I want to be? Think about things you enjoy, activities you might like to pursue, classes you might like to take. Think about your strengths and weaknesses, not just from an employer's point of view, but also from yours and your family's. What would you like to change about yourself? What makes you happy about yourself?

Take this opportunity, while you're thinking about who you are and what you want, to internalize the truth that *you* can't be downsized. Your job can be taken away, yes. But you as a person, your worth as a person, cannot be changed by the loss of a job. Your worth does not fluctuate with your job status. Your feelings of self-esteem may get buffeted. But your worth and value as a person do not change, no matter what happens to you. If you think you're nothing just because you don't have a fat paycheck, think about the painters and sculptors and writers, penniless during their lifetimes, who did what they did because of an inner drive to do it. Does their financial status make them less worthy, less insightful, less able to affect those of us who partake in their work? Certainly not. Does their posthumous "discovery" and adulation make them more worthy than they were in life? Certainly not. You may not have the same inner drive that they did. But the point remains. Your worth does not vary with the work you do or the money you make, be it a lot or a little. For some of us, this is not an easy concept to swallow. But how incredibly crucial it is for you to believe in yourself and support yourself. No one else can do that for you, even if they want to.

For some people, a layoff may be the best way to get focused on that long view that's so necessary to following a fulfilling life journey. Maybe this is the good news about downsizing—to recognize that life is so unpredictable that you really don't know whether this or any event is a crisis or an opportunity. Maybe one day you'll look back and be thankful for your layoff.

It's Not Over

And that's the whole point, after all. No one can judge a life until it's over. If you find yourself saying or thinking things like, "I'm a failure" or "I'll never find another job at my age" or "I'll never amount to anything," you're heading for trouble. You're making a sweeping conclusion about yourself and your life before your life is over. You're giving up in the middle of the race. You're rendering a verdict before all the evidence has even been created.

The fact of the matter is that you don't know what's going to happen next. You may meet an entrepreneur on an elevator and get a fabulous job with a new company. Maybe you'll take a class to build your computer skills and meet your future spouse there. Maybe you'll find a new job that makes you glad you lost your old one. You just can't predict the next event.

In my observation, however, the people most likely to encounter opportunities are the people who are looking for them and expecting them—people who know that life's not over until it's over, and that until then, you have to keep trying. I have a religious friend who says, "Coincidences happen more often when I pray about them." I think this is a good instinct, whether you look at it from a religious viewpoint or not. If you're prepared for luck and ready to accept good fortune, I think you're more likely to find it. But it's up to you to keep looking. If you're like most people, you've come through tough times before. You can weather this too. Just keep your eyes on that long view and head for the bright spot.

PART III

Family Matters

15

Bringing Work Home

AS IF THE EFFECT on individual workers weren't enough, anyone with loved ones knows that workplace anxiety comes home at night. It ripples across entire families, creating stress, inciting arguments, worsening worries about the future. This result is inevitable. Our families see us as we really are. When we're out of sorts, edgy and irritable, they're the first to know it. We affect and alter each other. We live in the same space. We know the meaning of fleeting facial expressions, silences, sighs, and outbursts. All in all, our families provide a pretty good barometer of the pressure in the household.

In many American families today, the barometer is rising. This should be no surprise. Scads of people have been laid off, nearly all with families at home dreading the bad news. Many millions more are worried, on the brink, poised for the day when the layoffs get personal. Our increasingly high-tech workplace tends to worsen the problem, because now you can bring work home in a more profound way than ever. Each person now has the potential to become a round-the-clock mobile office, connected to work by pagers, modems, and fax machines. A growing number of us have offices at home. These "advancements" give our families a direct connection to the source of our anxiety. And they can contribute to our collective troubles. After all, you and your family are in the same boat. If you're being rocked by a storm, they are too.

Studies already show some evidence of the rocking. Several have found the divorce rate about 50 percent higher in families where the husband loses his job and has trouble finding a new one. Another study suggests that laid-off workers are more likely to commit violence than people who are employed. Clearly, the changing American workplace is contributing to the struggles of America's families.

There's another factor, too, that I don't think we should ignore: the impact of changes coming from within the family itself. We have to recognize that "family" no longer has the neat and tidy definition it did a few decades ago. In fact, the typical nuclear family—mom, dad, and their biological kids—is no longer the most common form of the American family. These days, families come in all shapes and sizes. The definition can hardly be more specific than *two or more people related by blood or living arrangement*. Families are more of a hodgepodge than ever. Rarely any more is there a single breadwinner and a single homemaker. Many families are scrambling to make enough money to live; the housework gets done whenever it can. Many married adults have been married before. This leads to more and more "melded" families who face the added stresses of ex-wives, ex-husbands and the sometimes touchy relationships with stepchildren in addition to biological children. Today's families involve stepparents, stepchildren, mixed religions, mixed races, homosexual relationships, bisexual relationships, and, more and more often now, a single parent trying to raise children alone.

So when I say family, I mean nuclear family if it applies. But I also mean whatever it looks like in your family, under your roof. You'll notice that this chapter uses the word *spouse* a lot. If you have a boyfriend, a girlfriend, a partner, a live-in, if you have another adult in your life whom you don't think of as "spouse," don't get hung up in the word. Just hear what the chapter has to say and use whichever parts of it apply to your situation.

For families of all kinds, worries seem to be increasing on all fronts, not just at work. We used to worry that our children would lose their lunch money to bullies. Now we worry that they'll be slashed with knives or shot with handguns on the schoolyard. We used to worry about when to let teens date without chaperones. Now we worry about whether they'll reach their teenage years before they have sex, and whether they'll protect themselves from potentially deadly diseases. We used to worry about whether extended family members would be available to babysit. Now we worry about whether our children get home safely, and how they occupy themselves while they're at home alone. For many families, these are frightening times for many reasons. Because of the massive changes taking place inside the family and in the environment all around, we need to be more flexible and tolerant of each other than ever. And we need to support each other, help each other, stand by each other as best we can. We need to stick tightly together in whatever family unit we have.

Fortunately, no matter what your family looks like from a sociological viewpoint, there are some things you can do to help yourself and your loved ones from a psychological viewpoint. You can help your family weather this crisis. And you can help your family function as well as it can during this anxious time. This chapter offers some ideas about how to do it.

A Team of Two

If your home is beset by worries about unemployment or possible unemployment, probably the most important key to getting your family through it intact is for the adults to stay on the same team. This team spirit can be expressed in very specific ways. For example, if your spouse complains repeatedly about work and you're tired of hearing it, don't make snippy remarks, like, "Well, just quit then."

This may be the easiest way for you to stop hearing the complaints, but it won't help your spouse at all. It won't give your spouse any sense of support. It won't offer a viable alternative. And it won't help your spouse feel heard. In fact, it minimizes and dismisses your spouse's problem. Maybe that's why those complaints keep coming up in the first place.

Here's another example. If your spouse gets laid off, don't assume that your spouse was at fault. And whatever you do, DO NOT suggest *out loud* that your spouse was at fault. People are hard enough on themselves without help from the person who supposedly is their most trusted ally. Plus, if your spouse feels blamed for what happened, you've probably closed whatever doors were open to meaningful conversation about it. As we've seen earlier, a layoff these days probably is no one person's fault. But even if your spouse had something to do with it, casting blame will not help to identify and solve the problem for the benefit of future jobs.

Likewise, if your spouse gets laid off, don't assume it's your fault either. And don't let your spouse suggest to you that it is. This layoff is not because you prevented your spouse from spending enough time at work. It's not because your kids are too loud for your spouse to concentrate. It's not because child care keeps your spouse up at night or your schedule requires too much shared housework. In our economy, layoffs typically result from much bigger issues than that. First of all, understand that your laid-off spouse feels terrible, like a failure, and is looking for something to do with those feelings. If they come your way, don't argue and don't take it personally. Just don't participate.

Underneath it all, understand that people often do not connect events with feelings. For example, an acquaintance of mine, a very smart woman, said to me one day that she didn't know why she felt so tired and drained. I happened to know that her much-beloved dog had died the previous day. But it didn't occur to her, a day later, that his death could be causing her feelings. We do this all the time. We tend not to associate the way we feel with the events happening in our lives. This is a faulty attempt to protect ourselves from our feel-ings. We put disturbing events on a shelf and pretend they won't af-fect us. But they do. And job loss can exert a major effect. At times, this tendency to separate events from feelings can be helpful, particu-larly in a crisis, when you have to keep functioning. But in general, it can leave a lot of emotion floating around with nowhere to go and nothing to attach itself to. So it can come out in illness, temper tantrums, sudden depression. If your spouse loses a job or fears the loss of a job, those feelings may come out in a variety of ways, some of them aimed at you or your children.

Using whatever examples arise in your house, the key to main-taining your team is to avoid blaming and accusing each other. Blam-ing and accusing are the surest weapons to use if you want to start a fight, especially if they're preceded by "you always" or "you never." But especially in light of all the anxiety in many American homes just now, starting a fight should be the last thing you want to do. Instead, make a pact to give up the mutual blaming. If you do, you'll be much better able to handle—together—the stresses of work and home, too little time, and too little money. Keep in mind that work-related problems can show up in any room of the house, and they can hitch a ride on almost any topic. So when you decide to stop blaming and accusing, make it apply to everything. You'll be surprised at how much pressure you can take off a relationship, and how many fights you can avoid, with this one change in behavior.

Be aware that sex is one area of life deeply affected by anger, anxiety, and other strong emotions. It's also an area of life where many of us tend to make assumptions and jump to conclusions about a partner's thoughts and feelings. At a time when job-related issues are creating strong emotions, these assumptions and conclusions can ag-gravate an already difficult situation.

If you're like most people, it's tough to be genuinely interested in sex when you're very angry or very sad. It's also tough to be inter-ested in sex when you feel beaten down and worthless. Don't forget that these are precisely the emotions created by being laid off or fear-ing that you will be. So it's not unusual for these emotions to manifest as loss of interest in sex or a temporary loss of ability to have intercourse. Although these emotions apply to men and women alike, they tend to be more obvious in a man, who may not be able to attain an erection or may not keep it long enough to ejaculate. This is the old mind-body connection coming to the surface again.

Many times, the spouse detects these emotions as a change in the normal routine or pattern. Say, for example, that you tend to have sex every Saturday morning and sometimes on Sunday. This isn't a plan or an agreement you've reached with your spouse. It just seems to happen that way. Then one Saturday your spouse gets up before you're awake, gets dressed, and starts working around the house. The same thing happens on Sunday, and on the following Saturday. Your pattern has been altered, your signals disrupted, and now you're beginning to feel personally rejected. To make matters worse, your spouse also seems more withdrawn and irritable than usual. You assume it has something to do with you, and you withdraw as well.

There are several psychological problems at work in this common scenario. But the most important one for the story at hand is this: Work-related emotions can and will affect your sex life. But they do not have to damage your relationship with your spouse. If your usual pattern of sexual activity changes, try not to jump to conclusions about your spouse's feelings or motivation. Try not to rely on assumptions. Especially if your spouse has been laid off, fears being laid off, or has great frustration and anguish on the job, try not to take it personally when those emotions pop up in the bedroom. Instead, talk. Confirm that workplace worries are monopolizing your spouse's emotional energy just now. And do your best to maintain a loving relationship even in these circumstances. Try to be warm and affectionate without being sexual. Touch each other. Talk to each other. Try to regain some sense of playfulness in your life and, in particular, in your sex life. If you do, you'll probably lighten those worries about work in addition to strengthening the bond between you.

Money is another hot button for many couples. If you're living

paycheck to paycheck and one of you gets laid off, the financial pressures may seem insurmountable. But if you stick together, on the
same team, you'll be best able to find workable solutions. Here's how.
First, don't feel guilty that you're living paycheck to paycheck. Keep
in mind that our society encourages us to spend everything we make
on newer and bigger and better stuff. Most of us do just that. It's understandable that we do. Second, *tell each other* not to feel ashamed for
living paycheck to paycheck. Tell each other that this is no one's fault.
If you're in this together, then it's important to support each other
through it. And finally, work together—with patience and love—to
solve your financial problems as best you can and hopefully stop living paycheck to paycheck. Say out loud that gaining wisdom is an
important part of life, and now it's time for us to learn something
new. It may be painful, but together we can do it. Talking about your
worst fears can take some of the demons out of them. Say out loud,
"If we have to move to a smaller house, we will. If we have to sell the
house and rent an apartment, we will. If we have to drive an older
car, we will. If we have to use public transportation, we will. We may
need to make some changes to get ourselves through this hard time.
But if we stick together and do the best we can, we'll get through this
as a family." In addition to doing this exercise together, do it separately. Do it as self-talk, when you're alone, to keep your resolve to
stay on the same team and get through this trying time together.

Another way to help yourselves weather this adversity together is
for each of you to be willing to reevaluate your role in the relationship, the family, and the home. I have a patient in what we used to
call a "traditional" nuclear family. He worked. His wife didn't. He
wouldn't think of doing housework. His wife wouldn't think of asking. But then he lost his job, and he had trouble finding another one.
As luck would have it, his wife had computer programming skills.
She was able to find a good job in this high-demand area, so he stayed
home to care for the kids. Their willingness to shift roles helped this
couple not only survive but thrive in a rapidly changing workplace.
The key to making this shift work, by the way, is the realization that

giving up responsibility for your former role means giving up some control over how your former tasks get accomplished. If you can accept that, you can thrive too.

Always keep in mind that your spouse's job crisis may give *you* an opportunity that could benefit your whole family. You may have the opportunity to look for a job, to develop new skills, to redefine your life, to learn new things. You may not have wanted this opportunity, but you have it. And you may find that, in the long run, it improves your life. That's not always the case, of course. You may feel that this "opportunity" wrecked your life. But maybe there are more important things in life than ease and comfort. Maybe learning and growing and gaining wisdom, advances that seem to happen most during times of adversity, are more important. Whichever part of the crisis-opportunity duo you feel enveloped in just now, try to keep a sense of humor about it. Try to be an optimist about it. Look for what you can gain from being forcefully changed. You'll probably find it.

If you have children, you know that pregnancy and child-rearing teach you limitations and redirection. Sometimes it helps to look at job loss in the same way. Once it happens, you can't go back. But if you go forward together in a new direction, you may find the process uniquely rewarding.

When to Confront

Being laid off affects everyone differently. Some people sail right through it. Some people start new businesses. Some people pick themselves up and look for new jobs. And some people have trouble. If your spouse gets laid off and has trouble recovering right away, don't panic. Everyone needs some time to mourn and work through the emotions produced by the event. Maybe your spouse needs a little more time than you thought. If you push this person too hard or too soon to act as if everything is fine, you may end up alienated and fighting instead of helping either one of you. Many times, the best way to avoid needless conflict is to simply give your spouse some space and support. You don't have to criticize, nitpick, give opinions, or make observations on everything that bothers you about the way your spouse handles difficulty. However, there may come a time when you shouldn't ignore the problem any more.

Remember those signs of clinical depression from chapter 8? If, in your opinion, your spouse is showing several of those signs, and has been for a couple of weeks or more, I'd suggest making an appointment with a psychiatrist. If your spouse is indeed in clinical depression, the problem may not lift without help.

The most common reactions may not be quite as serious as clinical depression, but they do have the potential to disrupt your relationship and your family's life rather profoundly. For example, you may notice that your spouse is using alcohol or other drugs more than usual. This is an attempt at self-anesthesia, and it happens commonly after an event—like a layoff—that affects self-esteem. But as we all know, this misguided attempt to feel better only makes the problem worse, sometimes much worse. Increased use of alcohol and drugs should alert you that your spouse is having trouble working through emotions. Say you come home from work to find your laid-off spouse sitting in front of the TV with six or eight empty beer cans on the coffee table. Usually, your spouse drinks no more than a beer or two a day. It's probably not necessary to say anything right away, but if this increased drinking begins to form a pattern, you'll need to confront your spouse about it.

Don't be afraid of that word "confront" or think of it as being synonymous with punishment or fighting. It just means talking honestly and calmly about your thoughts and feelings. So what do you do? Start talking, gently. Say something like, "Honey, you have every right to drink beer. But I can see that you're drinking more of it than usual, and earlier in the day than usual. That makes me think you're drinking more because you're unhappy. I'm just not sure how, ultimately, the beer is going to make you happier."

Hopefully, this kind of approach will spark an honest conversation that helps your spouse get some of those painful emotions out in the air, where it's easier for them to blow away. If not, if your spouse refuses to recognize the problem, then you may want to find out about support groups or therapy groups in your area and urge your spouse to begin attending one. Sometimes group therapy can make you look at something you don't want to look at. After all, it's hard to ignore 10 people who are all telling you the same thing.

For some people, outbursts of anger become more common after a layoff. Again, especially if you have children who could be traumatized by these tantrums, consider confronting your spouse during a quiet moment. Say something like, "I love you, honey. I know you're under a lot of stress right now. But you're getting so angry that it's upsetting the kids and making the whole house more stressful. This way of handling your feelings just isn't working. I'd really like it if you and I could work more like a team. When you push me away, I can't be there for you. And right now, you need me to be there for you—not because you're weak, but in the way players help each other on a team. Everyone works together and it helps them be successful as a group."

If this kind of approach doesn't help, and your spouse won't go to individual or group counseling, go together. Get some couples therapy. Your presence may help your spouse overcome the reluctance to go alone, and you'll probably learn some things yourself.

Another common reaction to a layoff involves turning your feelings about it onto other people. One version of this tendency is called projection. For example, I had a patient named Gwen whose husband began to belittle her frequently. To Gwen, it seemed as if he picked on her constantly. In fact, he was being downright mean. He hadn't always been like this, and she assumed that he was beginning to find her middle-aged body and mind less attractive. Already a little insecure about her fading beauty, Gwen began to withdraw from him.

It turns out that Gwen's husband, Doug, had taken a forced early retirement from his executive position at a major bank a number of weeks earlier. The couple had invested shrewdly over the years and had no worries about their financial future, so Gwen didn't think the early retirement would affect him all that much. I suspected Doug's job loss had something to do with their problem, so I asked if Doug would mind coming in with Gwen on her next visit. He did, and he confirmed my suspicion. In fact, Doug felt deeply devalued by the loss of his job. And when his anger about it drove Gwen away, he then projected those feelings of devaluation onto her. In other words, because Doug felt that his value had declined, he believed that Gwen thought the same thing. And her emotional retreat convinced him that she no longer found him attractive or capable. So this couple began to separate emotionally from each other based on false assumptions. This is a common problem, especially among people who don't recognize or talk freely about what they're feeling.

A similar problem is called displacement. This is the kick-the-cat syndrome. It's where you transfer your feelings from their real target to something else. Say, for example, that you're stressed and frustrated that your boss keeps increasing your workload and tightening your deadlines. But you're afraid you'll lose your job if you complain about it. If your frustration is too powerful for you to work through on your own, you may choose instead to shout at other drivers on the freeway, snap at your loved ones, kick the cat, and so on. You're angry at your boss, not them. But because you can't yell at your boss, you displace those feelings onto someone or something else. Obviously, this can be harmful to relationships that are important to you. A better option would be to think about what's really making you angry, talk with your spouse or best friend about it, and get it out in a more acceptable way, like vigorous exercise. By the way, women may be more likely to come home depressed rather than angry, but the solution is the same. Talk with a trusted friend or loved one, don't hide away, and move your body.

The Best Medicine

The main message in all of this is that you and your loved ones are, in a certain sense, like explorers on a journey at sea. You're trying to make progress toward a general destination far away. And from time to time, a storm gathers around you that has the potential to capsize your boat. Especially in these stormy times, it's important for you adults to work together, helping and supporting each other, to keep from getting blown off course, or worse. Have you ever tried to row a boat with only one oar? All you do is go around in circles. If two of you have oars, but you're rowing in opposite directions, you go in even smaller circles. So if you want to make progress—in this case, increased emotional skills, added contentment, a stronger relationship, and so on—learn how to pull together. Teamwork is the ticket to progress.

How can you do that? Start by talking to each other, supporting each other. Never be ashamed of getting laid off. If you committed adultery or embezzled from the company, then maybe you should be ashamed. But especially if you lost a job in America in the 1990s, you have nothing to be ashamed about. It's almost a badge of your time. Don't be afraid. Just talk about how you're feeling. Respect each other's feelings. Listen to what your spouse is really saying. Invoke that emotional intelligence we talked about in chapter 6. Let yourself and your spouse talk about real emotions. They won't hurt you. And talking about them helps them go away.

I've heard people say you should try to leave your emotions about work at work. Or leave them in the car when you get home. Or push them out of your mind somehow and, at home, act like nothing is bothering you. Perhaps for some people at some times this is a good idea, especially if you're cranky about a relatively minor thing that you really don't need to disrupt your family over. That's fine. Just let it go. But if you're worried about losing your job, or you're truly unhappy in your job, I think leaving those feelings at work is a bad idea. I think you need to take them home. That's what having a family is about: bringing it home to people who love you. That's what a family should allow you to do.

A warning though: I'm talking about coming home honest, not abusive. If you come home angry all the time—throwing things, slamming doors, kicking the cat—your family will not stick with you emotionally. Your behavior will turn them off no matter how much they love you, and they won't want to participate in solving the family's issues with you. They're not going to want to help. Through exercise or therapy, you have to eventually get rid of the emotions that are pent up in there without dumping them continuously on your loved ones and closest friends. After all, how much fun is it to be around someone who's always angry?

You may have to work at developing a team spirit with your spouse, especially if you're both anxious about jobs, money, the future, the bills. This is hard stuff. But I can guarantee that you'll do better if you can find a way to support each other and talk honestly and lovingly with each other. Try going out as a couple once every week or two. It will give you time to reconnect, away from the hubbub and routines of home life. If you can, I'd also suggest going away with your spouse overnight every month or two, for the same reason. These tactics can help you keep your perspective. They can help you see and believe that you can get through this tough time together, just like you've gotten through tough times together in the past. This is the real bedrock truth, and you *can* support each other in it.

16

No Kidding Around

ON FIRST GLANCE, it might seem odd, in a book about career success, to find an entire chapter devoted to children. Frankly, I think this is part of our problem. For some reason, we Americans try desperately to separate the emotional parts of our lives into neat little compartments. Then we try to manage each one separately from the others. But life doesn't work that way. In fact, all of our little compartments melt together, and our emotions slop rather freely from one compartment to the next. So while it may seem that doing your job has nothing to do with raising your kids, your *reactions* to your job, and to America's job crisis in general, have everything to do with how your will kids grow up, how they cope with problems and setbacks, how they feel about their abilities and talents, what they think life owes them, and how they eventually involve their own spouses and kids in their personal problems. Like it or not, your working life affects your kids.

Even very young kids pick up subtle moods and messages from their parents. They may not know precisely how to define those moods or interpret those messages, but they still internalize their reactions to what they can sense about your feelings. So even if you never talk about your work-related struggles with your kids, they'll still grow up with feelings about work. And those feelings will be based largely on what they internalized from you. Instead of letting your kids develop half-interpreted, half-understood feelings about the role of work in one's life, wouldn't it be better to actually talk about it? Wouldn't it be better to involve your kids, in appropriate ways, in your thoughts and decisions about work? Wouldn't it be better to help your kids come to their conclusions about work *on purpose?*

Don't forget that work is way more than just a job. How your kids feel about work will color—perhaps define—their thoughts about success, fulfillment, what makes a happy life, what's truly important, and what isn't. The lessons you can teach your kids by opening your working life to them are astonishing in their depth and their breadth. We all know that raising kids is far more than kid stuff. But by relating honestly with them, helping them understand the personal importance of work, and—by your words and actions—teaching them what to value most in life, you can help your kids develop a healthy view of work and responsibility, and give them a good foundation on which to build their own vision of success.

An Honest View

All parents want to see their children succeed. But as we've discovered so clearly in the past few years, the American workplace is issuing no guarantees. No longer can you bundle your kids off to school knowing that, as soon as they graduate, they'll embark on that steady job or successful career. All you can do is prepare your kids as best you can to make wise decisions, overcome setbacks, and recognize opportunities in an uncertain and rapidly changing future. You can do that by showing them and involving them, directly and consciously, in your own process.

How much should you tell your kids about America's job crisis, your reactions to it, and your fears about your own future? Well, that depends. It depends on the ages of your kids. And it depends on how calmly you can talk about your emotions. Certainly, if you're terrified about what's ahead for you and your family, that's not something you want to dump on your kids. You don't want to show your children that you're terrified. Kids never want to see their parents without hope. It panics them. Then they feel like they have to become the parent and save the family ship. That's a big burden. And it's a burden that a kid shouldn't have to bear.

In a general sense, however, your kids probably already know something about how you feel. If you're nervous, your kids know something's up. If you're angry, your kids certainly know it. If you're feeling insecure, your kids have probably observed your reactions to that insecurity. But here's the danger. Kids tend to assume that they have something to do with their parents' feelings. So when you're tight-lipped, snappish, upset, angry, or whatever you are at your house, your kids are going to have a gut reaction to it, possibly a fearful reaction to it. Underneath it all, they may feel somehow responsible for your feelings. And they won't really know what to do with their reaction. They won't have the tools they need to solve this emotional puzzle adequately unless you clue them into what's happening with you. Then take them with you as you find your way through the maze.

So the first rule is this: If you have a problem, don't pretend everything's fine. Kids can see through your disguise, and they'll make up their own reasons for your problem. Instead, you need to find an age-appropriate way to explain your family's situation to your children and involve them in the solutions.

The second rule is this: Flank any discussion of a problem with reassurance that your family can and will stick together to get through it. Emphasize to your kids that the most important thing you have is each other.

The third rule is this: DO NOT teach your kids—unwittingly, by your moods, your actions, or your complaints —that life is unfair and that, yes, we should be angry about that. If you're stuck in feeling that life has been unfair to you, go back and read the first two sections of this book again. Find a way to change your mind about life's unfairness. For your family's sake, find a way to move forward, look for solutions to your problems, make the most of what you have, stop blaming other people for your station in life. Err on the side of generosity and forgiveness when you analyze other people's motives and behavior. Give them the benefit of the doubt. Then you can resume this discussion with your kids in a way that's helpful for them personally and for their futures in this world.

Together We Can

If you or your spouse have lost a job, or you think you might, or you hate the job you have, try to prepare your children ahead of time for possible emotional repercussions in your household. Try to shield your children from extreme or uncontrolled emotions whenever possible. But clue them in. Let them know that Mom and Dad are upset because something that's happening at work is hard to handle. Tell them that the family needs to stick together during this difficult time. Make sure all the children know that moments of tension, unhappiness, and adversity are normal parts of life. Urge older kids to cut Mom and Dad some slack because things are kind of hard right now. And emphasize the solidarity of the family. Tell your kids that you'll get through this tough time most successfully if you all pull together. Finally, make sure they know that they have not, in any way, caused the work-related problems your family faces.

Maybe it will help to put your situation in this context. Explain to your children that when you get a raise or a bonus at work, the whole family benefits from it. Likewise, when you meet adversity, the whole family meets it together. Tell them not to be surprised or overly angry about meeting adversity, because this is life, after all. This is the real world. We have no reason to expect that everything will always go our way. And right now, things are changing fast in the work world and we may have to make some changes that are better for our future. Tell your children that you don't know what the work world will be like by the time they're old enough to work. Maybe it will be easier to find and keep good jobs. Maybe it will be harder. We don't know. All we know is that, right now, lots of people are losing their jobs because lots of companies are changing directions. Explain that, in some ways, these big companies are like your family. They want to find the best way to do well, now and in the future. Above all, emphasize that every life has hard cycles and easy cycles. And that, in the hard cycles, it helps a lot for everyone to stick together and work together to get through it okay.

One of the keys to navigating this process successfully with your kids is to work through your issues in front of them. This is hard for many parents, but it's the only way your kids will learn to cope with their own problems. So parents, let the emotions go both ways. Tell your kids that you're not perfect. Tell them that sometimes they may have to say, "Dad, you're complaining," or "Mom, I thought you said this wasn't your boss's fault." Tell them that sometimes you might seem angry, but that they shouldn't worry that you're angry at them. Tell them not to be afraid to ask you about it. Tell them that sometimes, when you do get angry at them for something they did, you might get more angry than they think they deserve. Maybe they deserved only a third of it and the rest is for your boss at work. Let them ask you about that, too, and be willing to really look at your reaction. Let them remind you about the person you told them you want to be. Have enough respect for your kids and their intelligence that you're willing to interact with them on an honest emotional level that's appropriate for their ages.

If your children ask you some hard questions, give them the best, most honest answers you can. They may ask questions like, "Does this mean I won't get a car?" or "Will I still be able to go to summer camp this year?" Tell them you're sorry, but you just don't know. Tell them you wish you could control the situation. Tell them you really want to be able to give them their hearts' desires. Tell them they might need to pitch in and help, in age-appropriate ways. But sometimes, even when people do the best they can, it's impossible to see right away how things are going to work out. Don't ever make your kids sorry that they asked you a question, no matter how hard it is to find a good answer. If they don't feel free to ask you all their hard questions, they're almost certainly going to ask them of someone else —someone whose answer you may not like, someone who may not have your kids' best interests at heart. As part of your answer to all questions about work-related problems, be sure to emphasize to your kids that, whatever comes along, you'll handle it as a family, together.

If you're like most parents, you may find yourself feeling ashamed, maybe even like a failure, if you can't give your kids everything they ever wanted. And you might worry that those few outbursts fueled by work but unleashed on your kids will scar them for life. I wouldn't worry terribly much about that. On some level, I think we all understand that everything in life has a harmony and a balance. If you've been a good parent in general, and you hit a period of time when you can't be a good parent, your kids will, in all likelihood, be fine. If their lives have been basically nurtured and supported, if they know they've been loved, it'll be okay. A few periods of difficulty with a parent won't harm a child permanently. It's more important to look at the pattern of a lifetime. What kind of patterns have your kids internalized from you? What kind of messages do they hear and see over and over again from you? These are the important questions. In fact, if your children can go through a hard period of time with you—even if you're *not* the perfect parent throughout— they'll get to see you work through problems. Maybe they'll see you change your financial habits. Maybe they'll see you go talk to a mental health professional to work through things. Maybe they'll see you get rid of a fancy new car and replace it with an older, cheaper car. They'll learn coping skills of their own as a result. If you can just maintain your emphasis that the family is most important, they're very likely to get through even your darkest moments with you.

One way to help children feel safe and cared for, even if you're not functioning at your normal level, is to remind your children of how many people are out there in the world to help your family. If you have an extended family and good friends, talk about their availability and their support. Go visit them, and invite them over, on a regular basis. As much as possible, make your children feel like they're part of a huge network of safety. Help your children see and believe that people can and will help each other in times of need. The indirect benefit of doing this, of course, is that your children will want to help other people as well. Perhaps they can start right where they are, in your family.

Helping Hands

One of the best ways to help children feel like they're part of a supportive team is to let them help. In general, kids love to help. In farm families, they get that chance all the time. But in places where we work primarily in offices and shops and businesses outside of our homes, that's not so true. So maybe this is another opportunity in the midst of our crisis. Maybe we can help our children build some self-esteem by letting them help, in age-appropriate ways, in the family's time of need. Maybe they can start a paper route. Maybe they can sell lemonade. Maybe they can help with chores around the house. One of the best options is to work together, as a family. Have a family work day, and give each child an age-appropriate task to complete. Then, when everyone finishes, do something together, like a picnic lunch. The issue is not about generating income, but about helping the family get through a tough time together. When kids feel that they can make a contribution of themselves, of their time and effort, they learn a very valuable lesson. They learn they can make a difference. And in so learning, they develop self-esteem.

This approach may be most beneficial, ironically, in families who are relatively well off. A fair number of children in affluent families suffer from a sense of purposelessness that can eventually lead to unacceptable behaviors. Helping parents get through a difficult period can not only teach pampered kids some survival skills, it can also help these kids feel grateful for what they have. It also helps to enforce self-discipline in these kids, even if their parents have trouble setting economic limits. Working together, and pitching in to help, can teach kids a valuable lesson, whether the family's income is threatened or not.

In addition to feeling that they're helping the family, kids may form some valuable thoughts about their own futures as well. For example, I had a patient who bought a desktop printing and copy franchise after losing his well-paid job, and he pressed his family into service to make the new business run. His teenage son was charged with delivering the orders. After a few months at this job, the young man figured out that he didn't want to spend his life driving around with a car full of paper stock. As a result, he has become much more motivated to do well in school and prepare himself for a challenging career. He experienced the alternative, and he didn't like it. This was an excellent lesson for him to learn and an excellent age at which to learn it.

By example and by opportunity, parents in this day and age must teach children some kind of work ethic: that if you try hard, you can still overcome adversity. Recognize that teens may have their own anxieties about future success. One of the most important lessons you can teach these children is the lesson of lifelong learning. Help your children figure out how to learn, and give them confidence that they can learn. Letting them find ways to help is a good start.

Time for Kids

No one knows better than a parent that there's a lot to teach our kids, and not many years of childhood available for teaching. And since most parents work these days, we have to balance the thorny issue of where and how to spend our limited amount of time. I can't tell you the best way to portion out your time among your family, your work, and everything else that's important to you. You're the only one who can do that for yourself. What I can do, however, is offer you some ideas that might help you arrive at a solution that's reasonable for you.

First, think about how much time you do spend with your children. Do you know? Most parents spend something like three hours with their kids on weekdays, and around eight hours with them on weekends. About two-thirds of parents worry that's not enough time. Are you one of them?

Second, think about how you spend the time you do have with your kids. Are you reading with them? Are you talking with them? Are you playing with them? Are you helping them with homework? Or are you simply in the same house with them, or maybe watching the same television with them?

If you're like many parents, you probably skipped right over that question, "Are you playing with them?" After all, kids get plenty of play time with siblings, with friends, and during school activities. But for your kids' sake and your own sake, don't skip that question. Don't fail to participate in this crucial aspect of your child's development. Especially for kids under 10 years old, play is the primary avenue by which they express their feelings and work through their problems. They don't know this is happening, and you may not either. But it is. Think about it. Children are largely controlled by the adults who raise them. So, in games and play, children can create a universe of their own, where they can be in control, make decisions, take actions, observe the effects of those actions, and—perhaps most important—express their feelings and emotions. Through games and playing, children master many of the emotions and skills required for living successfully as grown-ups. They learn to express their feelings appropriately. They learn coping skills. They gain a sense of their own creativity, initiative, preferences, and accomplishment. They gain a sense of themselves.

That's why it's so important to play with your kids. It gives you an entry into their world, where you can watch them and interact with them at their own level. But please keep one thing in mind. This is *playing*. This is not lesson time or lecture time. It's not another opportunity for you to control your child's activities. And it's not about teaching a child to win. Playing isn't about winning or losing. Playing is about letting go, having fun, laughing. It's not a purposeful activity. Playing is its own justification. You don't want to work hard at playing. You want to have fun. Besides helping you relate better with your kids, playing probably will also help you. Many of us have grown up to be very serious adults, and these scary economic times have only made us more serious. So my advice is to lighten up. Play with your children. If you don't have any, borrow some from your friends or extended family. Let those children teach you how to relax and have fun.

Third, if you think you're spending too much time at work, think about why that might be. Are you worried about losing your job if you spend less time there? Are you fighting with your spouse so much that it's easier to simply check out and spend your time at work? Is it just habit to spend every waking hour at work? If work takes up more of your life than it should, people have probably told you to just cut back. Just come home at five o'clock. Just stop working so hard. This is a very simplistic approach that may frustrate you more than it helps you. Unless you need the income just to survive, what you should do is look at *why* your job takes up so much of your life. Maybe it makes you feel productive, successful at something, worthwhile. So the real reason you spend too much time at work may have nothing to do with your employer's expectations or what's happening at home. It may be that you're relying too much on work to give you a sense of personal worth. If this could be the case, it's important for you to spend time thinking about what's really important to you and what you want to base your life satisfaction on. Whatever you decide, it has to be something you can live with, and your kids can live with.

Above all, understand that you can't say one thing to a kid and do something else. What kind of lesson does that teach? Instead, you have to decide for yourself what's most important in your life, and live that way. For some parents, it means facing the fact that they may not live up to the financial bounty they dreamed about. If this is you, you have to reevaluate how important those dreams are, in light of the children whose lives you hold in your hands. Once you begin to more clearly understand your feelings about these concepts, then you can decide what to do about the amount of time you spend at work and at home.

Building Values

Much of what we've just been talking about gets at your personal values—what you think is most important, and how that thinking establishes and alters your behavior. We complain all the time in this country that we don't have enough values. Well, here's our chance to teach our kids something about values. About honesty. About trying hard so you can be proud of yourself, not so you can make a million dollars. About being part of a team and using your mental and physical abilities to help your loved ones. About not blaming people for your situation. About taking responsibility for yourself. About deciding what's really important in life. This hardship that we face in the job world right now can teach us valuable lessons in every area of life, if we let it. It can give us a way to teach our kids that they're valuable people; there's no better route to solid self-esteem than that.

It's up to you as a parent to give your children the sense that they can do almost anything they want, if they're willing to work at it with discipline and patience. You can do this by saying so. You can do it by example. Take my father, for example. He married at age 20 and had his first child—me—by the time he was 21. In his mid-20s, he decided to start lifting weights. He worked and he worked and eventually, at age 28, he broke weight-lifting records. Later in life, he decided to go back to school. Because he had only a vocational degree, he started by earning his academic high school diploma. Then he went on to get an undergraduate degree. And then, at age 67, he got a masters. Not only that, but he got straight As. And I watched him do it. What my father did gave me a very clear idea—a conviction, really—that if you make up your mind, there isn't anything you can't do. I watched it happen.

Keep in mind that this is a subtle and complex message. Be careful not to superimpose your own definition and desire for success on your children. And be careful not to establish such unrealistic expectations for them that you set them up for failure. But in general, seeing examples like the one I saw in my father makes you feel empowered to realize even major accomplishments. It doesn't matter whether they're major accomplishments by the world's standards or by your own standards. The effect is still the same.

My father taught me another valuable lesson as well. During the periods of time when he was out of work, he used the opportunity to spend time with me. We went to museums. We went to libraries. From him I learned that you can make the most of opportunities, even opportunities that tend to produce fear and anger.

If you put your mind to it, you can teach your children—by example and explanation—to set a value system and stay true to it, to adapt to change while retaining that value system, to be willing and able to continuously acquire skills, to be able to observe and evaluate the world around them. These skills are critically important, especially now. One of the first issues you may find yourself faced with is the "fairness" issue. If your family has to cut back on some things to survive, you're almost sure to hear one of your kids say, "This isn't fair. My friends have..." You finish the sentence. Your kids' friends are going to have cars, games, bicycles, cable TV, whatever. Keep in mind that your best and most important opportunities to talk about values-oriented issues will probably come along with difficult, emotionally-charged questions and problems. Now's your chance. In fact, every time a hard issue like this comes up, you have a chance to reflect the kind of values you think are important, those you want your kids to have.

Always take a moment to think before you answer a child's complaint or address a child's problem. Don't ever dismiss a child's concerns. Don't minimize them. Take a moment to think about the problem from the child's point of view. Forget about your own stuff for a minute, and respond accordingly. On the fairness complaint, for example, you could say something like, "I'm sorry honey. I know you really want that new stereo, but I want you to think about something for a minute. Many of the people in the world live their whole lives without a stereo. There are lots of people in the world who don't even have a bike or a bedroom. They don't have anything. Let's talk about fair. To lots of kids around the world, it sure isn't fair that we have a TV, a VCR, air conditioning, and a whole house just for us. That's not fair either. We'll do the best we can to get you a stereo. But it may take longer than we thought. And it may mean that you'll have to help pay for it too. In the meantime, it's really important to realize how much we already have. It's important not to get stuck on that word *fair*." Certainly, this is not the answer your child wanted, and you probably won't get a warm response at the time. But remember that when possessions have to be earned, they grow in perceived value. And if you establish a pattern of responses like this one, they'll come back to serve your child in the future. I can guarantee it.

It's also important to teach your children life-enhancing values, like compassion and empathy. There's no better way to do that than by action. Take the whole family to the soup kitchen for a couple of hours. Take them to the food bank with you when you take a box of food. Have your child find a toy or two to donate to needy children. These kinds of activities will remind your kids that there are lots of people out there, and that they live in a very wide variety of circumstances. It won't be long before your kids get the idea that they have a relatively good life. They may have to revise their definition of what a good life is. But this is the key they need. The ability to look at their lives in perspective. You'll do them a great service if you can help them understand that the way you feel about things springs from the way you view them. Then help them understand that every person looks at life through his or her own personal lens. And that every person has some control over the direction and focus of that lens.

Home Fires

In this time of workplace worry, sometimes it might be nice to think that our children don't really need our full attention, that they'll get by okay even if we don't give them our all as parents. After a long day of stress and anxiety on the job or pounding the pavement, it may feel as though there just isn't any more to give. But I want to tell you something. You and your kids will both be better off if you can dredge down just a little deeper. Find the energy you need to really *love* your kids. Find the time to read them one more story. Find the desire to put down that newspaper and pick up that baseball. From a mental health perspective, your kids may turn out to be different people if you do. You will too.

Never forget that the first school a child ever attends is the home school. Some people will tell you that children learn more in that first school than they do for the rest of their years put together. Certainly, it's the most important school we attend. It gives us our sense of how people relate to one another, how people relate to us, what's important and what's not, what behavior is acceptable and appropriate, what's valued and what's not. The home school has the opportunity to give kids their original, irreplaceable feelings of being worthy and lovable and capable. They learn about self-discipline and delayed gratification. From these early years, children form a set of assumptions about life and other people that last into and throughout their adult lives.

If you don't get what you need in the beginning, in that first school, you grow up with emotions and assumptions that may create problems for you later in life. I see some of these people as patients, people who seek out someone like me to help them reformulate their thinking patterns. But you can never completely erase what formed as a result of not getting what you needed when you were a little child. You can never go back and repeat your early childhood the way you can go back and repeat a grade in school.

I'm not telling you this to suggest that you need to be a perfect parent or that you have to do everything "right" for your children. This is an impossible standard that too many parents, especially mothers, try to achieve. Don't do that. Just remember that what adults believe about all aspects of life—yes, even work—come largely from what they embraced or rejected as children. By giving your children the love and support and discipline they need, along with important tools for adapting to our changing world, you can accomplish a parent's most important goal. You can set your children up for success, real success, no matter what happens in their future.

17

Community Ties

T HERE WAS A TIME in our country's history when we tried to stick together. We lived in close communities. We knew each other. We called local children by name and walked freely along darkened streets. We wouldn't think twice about helping a neighbor in need. But when personal levels of stress and fear and anger are on the rise, our tendency is to turn inward. It's human nature. We want to protect our families and ourselves. We become less giving, less willing to help when we're worried about someone or something being out to get us. We tend to turn our backs on our communities, leaving them to get along without us while we take care of our own needs. Naturally, our communities suffer.

At this time, when many of us are worried about surviving our workplace worries, that's exactly what's happening. Our communities and our neighbors are suffering. And I fear that we face a real and dire risk—a risk that, if we let our fears about work and money take over, we'll continue to turn away more and more from community needs. It's understandable that we should do just that. After all, when you know that your economic system is shaky, you almost can't help but be less generous. You cut down on the spontaneous little gifts you used to buy. You stop giving money to the man who stands on your corner holding a sign. You don't feel as free to give a spur-of-the-moment donation or a few hours to the telethon on a Saturday afternoon. The fear of losing a job and a lifetime of accomplishment changes people, and I can understand why.

The fear also makes us more irritable, more anxious, less apt to give our neighbors a break. You see it on the freeways. You see it in the grocery store. We're impatient. We're unforgiving. We're unwilling to go a step or two out of the way to help a stranger who obviously needs it. We're afraid. We pin blame for our troubles on other members of what used to be the community. I read the papers and listen to the news, just like you do. I can understand why we act this way.

People who feel unstable in their lives and routines also have difficulty making commitments to ongoing community activities. If you think you're going to have to move out of town or launch a job search or sell your house, or if you're working two jobs just to get by, becoming a scout leader or a school board member probably is not high on your list. I can understand why.

The way we're acting as a nation of communities is perfectly understandable, given our fears about a potentially unemployed or underpaid future. There's just one problem. The way we're acting will only make matters worse. It's backfiring. And so we end where we began, with a truth that seems to contain contradictory elements. Now, when we feel most threatened, is perhaps the most important time to look outward, to get past ourselves and think about someone else. We need to overpower our fears and our sense that life is cruel and unfair and unpredictable. Yes, maybe that's all true. But concentrating on those feelings, giving in to them, building your lifestyle on them, will only make you bitter and alone. By your own actions, you will have created the life you feared, living behind high walls and barred windows to protect yourself from your estranged community. You know, the most dangerous person in the world is a person who has nothing to lose. So the more we abandon the less fortunate members of our communities to their fate, the more likely we are to continue creating a society plagued by desperation, hate, and crime.

One of the messages that should have trumpeted loud and clear from this book is that your reality is as you see it and your future is what you make it. Not in the financial sense, perhaps, or in the perks you're awarded at work. You may not be able to influence those. No, I'm talking about something much more important. I'm talking about the effect created by your attitude, your expectations, your values, your assumptions about life and the people around you. I'm talking about benefits that accrue to *you* when you engage in something, anything, that helps pull you out of your focus on your own troubles. Coincidentally, your community benefits as well.

I'm not suggesting that our communities are breaking down solely because of our worries about work. But it's certainly a factor. When we enter that insular state where all we can think about is protecting our own, we quickly lose sight of the big picture. We get self-involved. We lose our ability to empathize with people outside our small circle of family and friends. We buy into the us-and-them mentality. And the community suffers. Does any of this sound familiar?

So what should we do? We can't put the stability back into the economic picture. We can't guarantee high-paying jobs for all. We can't foresee an end to this difficult and nervous time. So our only alternative is to look for that pony. What do you have to lose? Maybe helping someone else will show you how good you really have it. Maybe acting on what's really important in life will help you see the pettiness of worrying about your next big purchase. Maybe letting go of your anxiety for a moment will show you the folly of trying to control your future. And maybe, just maybe, you'll find yourself becoming more satisfied with your life—and yourself—than ever before. Now you've found a kind of success that never goes away.

ACKNOWLEDGMENTS

THE AUTHORS WISH TO THANK:

Janet Westberg, whose unflagging faith made this book possible.

Lenore Terr, who served as a role model and generous source of information.

Danny and Hillary Goldstein, who have supported this book from the beginning.

Connie Warren, for remarkable insight and unfailing encouragement.

RESOURCES AND READINGS

RESOURCES FOR MENTAL HEALTH

National Depressive and Manic-Depressive Association
730 N. Franklin Street, Suite 501
Chicago, IL 60610
(800) 826-3632

National Foundation for Depressive Illness, Inc.
P.O. Box 2257
New York, NY 10116
(800) 245-4340

National Mental Health Association
1021 Prince Street
Alexandria, VA 22314
(800) 969-6642

Organization for Depression Awareness, Inc.
P.O. Box 898
Orange, CT 06477
(800) 799-0208

Internet Employment Sources

America's Job Bank
http:///www.ajb.dni.us/

Career Magazine
http://www.careermag.com

CareerMosiac
http://www.careermosiac.com

Careerpath.com
http://www.careerpath.com

E-Span
http://www.espan.com

Online Career Center
http://www.occ.com

Quest USA
http://www.questusa.com

Robert Half Financial and Information Systems Recruiting
http://www.roberthalf.com

The Monster Board
http://www.monster.com

MEET YOUR DOCTOR

To find out a little more about a physician you're interested in seeing, try a
service called Med-i-Net. It's the only organization approved by the American Medical Association to give you information from its huge physician
database. For a $15 fee ($5 for each additional name), you can find out
where a physician received training and licensure, what specialty the physician practices, what board certifications and other professional credentials
the physician has, and whether the physician has been disciplined in any
state. You can call Med-i-Net toll-free at (888) 275-6334, or use this Internet address: http://www.med-i-net.com.

Suggested Reading

Business and Economy

Barlett, D. L. 1992. *America: What Went Wrong?* Kansas City: Andrews and McMeel.

Drucker, P. 1994. *The New Realities: In Government and Politics/In Economics and Business/In Society and World View.* New York: Harper-Business.

Drucker, P. 1993. *Post-Capitalist Society.* New York: HarperBusiness.

Hamel, G. and C. K. Prahalad. 1994. *Competing for the Future.* Boston: Harvard Business School Press.

Hammer, M. and J. Champy. 1993. *Reeingeering the Corporation: A Manifesto for Business Revolution.* New York: HarperBusiness.

Hersey, P. and K. H. Blanchard. 1993. *Management of Organizational Behavior: Utilizing Human Resources.* Englewood Cliffs, NJ: Prentice Hall.

Kanter, R.M. 1995. World Class: *Thriving Locally in the Global Economy.* New York: Simon & Schuster.

Luttwak, E. 1993. *The Endangered American Dream: How to Stop the United States from Becoming a Third-World Country and How to Win the Geo-Economic Struggle for Industrial Supremacy.* New York: Touchstone.

Maddrick, J. 1993. *The End of Affluence: The Causes and Consequences of America's Economic Dilemma.* New York: Random House.

McElvaine, R. 1996. *What's Left? A New Democratic Vision for America.* Holbrook, MA: Adams Media Corporation.

Reich, R.B. 1992. *The Work of Nations: Preparing Ourselves for 21st-Century Capitalism.* New York: Vintage Books.

Reichheld, F. 1996. *The Loyalty Effect: The Hidden Force Behind Growth, Profits, and Lasting Value.* Boston: Harvard Business School Press.

Ruggiero, G. and S. Shakula, eds. 1993. *The New American Crisis: Radical Analyses of the Problems Facing America Today.* New York: The New Press.

Samuelson, R.J. 1995. *The Good Life and its Discontents: The American Dream in the Age of Entitlement (1945-1995).* New York: Times Books/Random House.

Thurow, L.C. 1996. *The Future of Capitalism: How Today's Economic Forces Shape Tomorrow's World.* New York: William Morrow and Company, Inc.

Downsizing

Meyer, G.J. 1996. *Executive Blues: Down and Out in Corporate America.* Franklin Square Press.

Moore, M. 1996. *Downsize This! Random Threats from an Unarmed American.* New York: Crown.

The New York Times. 1996. *The Downsizing of America.* New York: Times Books/Random House.

Job Search

Beyer, C., D. Pike, and L. McGovern. 1993. *Surviving Unemployment: A Family Handbook for Weathering Hard Times.* New York: Henry Holt and Company.

Bolles, R. N. 1996. *What Color is Your Parachute? A Practical Manual for Job-Hunters & Career-Changers.* Berkeley: Ten Speed Press.

Career Management Associates. 1997. *The Job Search Organizer.* New York: Hatherleigh Press.

Dent, H.S. 1995. *The Great Jobs Ahead: Your Comprehensive Guide to Surviving and Prospering in the Coming Work Revolution.* New York: Hyperion.

Dixon, P. and S. Tiersten. 1995. *Be Your Own Headhunter Online.* New York: Random House.

Kennedy, J. L. and T. J. Morrow. 1995. *Electronic Job Search Revolution.* John Wiley & Sons, Inc.

Krannich, R.L. and C.R. Krannich. 1995. *The Best Jobs for the 1990s and Into the 21st Century, 2nd edition.* Manassas Park, VA: Impact Publications.

Goodwin, M., D. Cohn, and D. Spivey. 1997. *Net Jobs.* Michael Wolff & Co. Publishing.

Gonyea, J.C. 1996. *The On-Line Job Search Companion.* New York: McGraw-Hill Self-Help.

Mental Health

Beck, Aaron. 1987. *Cognitive Therapy of Depression.* Guilford Press.

Benson, H. 1979. *The Mind/Body Effect: How Behavioral Medicine Can Show You the Way to Better Health.* New York: Simon and Schuster.

Burns, D. 1980. *Feeling Good: The New Mood Therapy.* New York: William Morrow and Company.

Coles, R. 1964. *A Study of Courage and Fear.* Boston: Little, Brown.

Coles, R. 1961. *The Mind State.* Boston: Atlantic Monthly Press/Little, Brown.

Damon, J.E. 1988. *Shopaholics: An 8-Week Program to Control Compulsive Spending.* New York: Avon Books.

Flach, Frederic. 1995. *The Secret Strength of Depression.* New York: Hatherleigh Press.

Gardner, H. 1993. *Multiple Intelligences: The Theory in Practice*. New York: Basic Books.

Gold, M. S. 1986. *The Good News About Anxiety*. New York: Villard Books

Gold, M. S. 1986. *The Good News About Depression*. New York: Villard Books.

Gold, M. S. 1989. *The Good News About Panic, Anxieties, and Phobias*. New York: Villard Books.

Gold, M. S. 1991. *The Good News About Drugs and Alcohol*. New York: Villard Books.

Goleman, D. 1995. *Emotional Intelligence*. New York: Bantam Books.

Gregory, R., ed. 1987. *The Oxford Companion to the Mind*. New York: Oxford University Press.

Healy, B. 1995 *A New Prescription for Women's Health: Getting the Best Medical Care in a Man's World*. New York: Viking.

Kaplan, H.I. and B.J. Sadock, eds. 1989. *Comprehensive Textbook of Psychiatry, volume 1, 5th edition*. Baltimore: Williams and Wilkins.

Klein, D.F. and P.H. Wender. 1993. *Understanding Depression: A Complete Guide to its Diagnosis and Treatment*. New York: Oxford University Press.

Mendelson, J. H. and N. K. Mello. 1985. *The Diagnosis and Treatment of Alcoholism*. New York: McGraw-Hill Book Co.

Reiser, M. S. 1984. *Mind, Brain, Body*. New York: Basic Books.

Selye, H. 1976. *The Stress of Life, revised edition*. New York: McGraw-Hill Book Co.

Seligman, M. 1991. *Learned Optimism*. New York: Knopf.

Swedo, S. and H. Leonard. 1996. *It's Not All In Your Head: Now Women Can Discover the Real Causes of Their Most Commonly Misdiagnosed Health Problems*. San Fransisco: HarperSanFrancisco.

West, L. J. and M. Stein. 1982. *Critical Issues in Behavioral Medicine*. Philadelphia: J.B. Lippincott.

Yalom, I. D. 1980. *Existential Psychotherapy*. New York: Basic Books.

Yalom, I. D. 1990. *Every Day Gets a Little Closer: A Twice-Told Therapy*. New York: Basic Books.

Work

Glassner, B. 1994. *Career Crash: America's New Crisis—and Who Survives*. New York: Simon & Schuster.

Karpel, C.S. 1995. *The Retirement Myth: What You Must Know Now to Prosper in the Coming Meltdown of Job Security, Pension Plans, Social Security, the Stock Market, Housing Prices, and More*. New York: HarperCollins Publishers.

Kinney, J.A. 1995. *Violence at Work: How to Make Your Company Safer for Employees & Customers*. Englewood Cliffs, NJ: Prentice Hall.

Kotter, J. P. 1995. *The New Rules: How to Succeed in Today's Post-Corporate World*. New York: The Free Press.

Levering, R. 1988. *A Great Place to Work: What Makes Some Employers So Good (And Most So Bad)*. New York: Random House.

Pelletier, K. R. 1984. *Healthy People in Unhealthy Places: Stress and Fitness at Work*. A Merloyd Lawrence Book.

Quittel, F. 1994. *Fire Power: Everything You Need to Know Before and After You Lose Your Job*. Berkeley: Ten Speed Press.

Reinhold, B. B. 1996. *Toxic Work: How to Overcome Stress, Overload, and Burnout and Revitalize Your Career*. A Dutton Book.

Rifkin, J. 1995. *The End of Work: The Decline of the Global Labor Force and the Dawn of the Post-Market Era*. New York: G.P. Putnam's Sons.

Schor, J. B. 1991. *The Overworked American: The Unexpected Decline of Leisure*. New York: Basic Books.

Senge, P. M. 1994. *The Fifth Discipline: The Art & Practice of the Learning Organization*. New York: Currency/Doubleday.

Sinetar, Marsha. 1987. *Do What You Love, The Money Will Follow*. Mahwah, NJ: Paulist Press.

Terkel, S. 1972. *Working: People Talk About What They Do All Day and How They Feel About It*. New York: Pantheon Books.

Yate, M. 1995. *Beat the Odds: Career Buoyancy Tactics for Today's Turbulent Job Market*. New York: Ballantine Books.

General

Adams, S. 1996. *The Dilbert Principle: A Cubicle's-Eye View of Bosses, Meetings, Management Fads & Other Workplace Afflications*. New York: HarperBusiness.

Carnegie, D. 1981. *How to Win Friends and Influence People, revised edition*. New York: Pocket Books/Simon and Schuster.

Csikszentmihalyi, M. 1996. *The Evolving Self: A Psychology for the Third Millenium*. New York: HarperPerennial.

Csikszentmihalyi, M. 1990. *Flow: The Psychology of Optimal Experience*. New York: HarperPerennial.

Elgin, D. 1993. *Voluntary Simplicity: Toward A Way of Life That Is Outwardly Simple, Inwardly Rich, revised edition*. New York: Quill/William Morrow.

Encyclopaedia Britannica, Inc. 1976. *The Annals of America, volume 10*. London: Encyclopaedia Britannica, Inc.

Frank, R. H. and P. J. Cook. 1995. *The Winner-Take-All Society*. New York: Penguin Books.

Hamblin, K. 1996. *Pick A Better Country: An Unassuming Colored Guy Speaks His Mind About America*. New York: Simon and Schuster.

Jensen, C. and Project Censored. 1996. *Censored: The New That Didn't Make the News and Why, 20th Anniversary edition*. Four Walls Eight Windows.

Lamott, A. 1994. *Bird by Bird: Some Instructions on Writing and Life*. New York: Pantheon Books.

McKnight, J. 1996. *The Careless Society: Community and Its Counterfeits*. New York: Basic Books/HarperCollins Publishers.

Peale, N. V. 1952. *The Power of Positive Thinking*. New York: Prentice-Hall.

In addition to these readings, *The New York Times,* the *Wall Street Journal,* and other major newspapers provide extensive daily coverage of economic and workplace issues.

INDEX